COLOR YOUR ROOM

How to stop being afraid of
color and use it with style

COLOR
YOUR ROOM

p

This is a Parragon Publishing Book
This edition published in 2003

Parragon Publishing
Queen Street House
4 Queen Street
Bath BA1 1HE, UK

Created and produced for Parragon by The Bridgewater Book Company Ltd.

Creative Director Stephen Knowlden
Art Director Colin Fielder
Designer Johnny Pau
Editorial Director Fiona Biggs
Editors Mark Truman, Sarah Yelling
Photography Alistair Hughes
Picture Researcher Lynda Marshall
Styling & Illustrations Stewart Walton

ISBN: 0-75257-167-2

Printed in China

Contents

Introduction   6

Color and Design   8

Textures and Effects   26

Color Highlights   44

Creating a Style with Color   56

Index   94

Acknowledgments   96

Introduction

Color is everywhere—and we are more aware of it than we realize. We take it very much for granted, but imagine what it would be like to only see our world in black and white? We would soon be yearning for some bright colors again. This book will help you look at colors with a decorator's eye and use them to make your home a happier, more comfortable, and more stylish place to live. It will also stop you being afraid of color!

ABOVE **Use of a bold color on nearly every surface may not appeal to everyone as a decorating option. If the color is applied with confidence, however, the results can be stunning, and certainly make a strong statement, often reflecting the personality of a room's occupant. This funky purple kitchen is enlivened by the clever use of light on the lime green wall, which reflects on the shiny surfaces.**

Right from a very young age, children are aware of their favorite colors. There is always a favorite red T-shirt or blue jumper that has to be worn over any other piece of clothing. As adults, this awareness is transferred to where we live and the colors we like to be surrounded with. A lot of children, however, also have very strong ideas about what color they want their bedroom walls to be! The aim of this book is to help you make color decisions that suit you and your lifestyle best. If, for example, you have a very stressful job, it's no good painting your bedroom bright red—calming aquamarines, lilacs, and shades of blue will help provide the right kind of atmosphere.

The first section of the book introduces color theory and explains the basics. All colors are derived from the three primary colors, red, yellow, and blue, from which there are then created the secondary colors of orange, green, and violet. There are also hints on creating an illusion—for example, painting your ceiling a darker color to visually lower it if it is very high— and planning your color schemes. This is often the most important part as decorating mistakes can be very costly to rectify, and, unless you have unlimited cash, you do need to get it right the first time.

The second section of the book discusses textures and effects, and introduces some projects to try out. It's all very well choosing a color scheme, but different textures and paint effects can stop that scheme looking flat and dull and will introduce some depth. The third section introduces the concept of color highlighting, which can also be used to provide interest and diversity in any decorating scheme.

The final section chooses some of the best-known decorating styles from around the world—English Country, Tuscany, and Moorish, to name but a few—and shows you how to bring that style into your home. There are felt appliqué curtains, if you fancy bringing a touch of the Romany into your home, and wonderful burnished gold Indian bindi stamps, to add that exotic element to any room. All of these projects—and in fact this whole book—are designed to introduce you to color and to give maximum impact for minimum effort. So pick a color you like and get painting!

BELOW **For the typical Tuscan look, use bright colors with a distinctive chalky finish. Ochers, umbers, and pistachio green look particularly good here, especially when contrasted with the rich-red rustic cupboard. These chalky Mediterranean paints fade to a wonderful soft color in the hot sun.**

ABOVE **Pink, orange, and peach tones can look fantastically lush in the right setting. Here, bright pink walls and lighter pink blinds contrast wonderfully with the warm clotted-cream shades of the upholstery and carpet. The warm ambient lighting mixed with natural light casts a wonderful rosy glow over the whole room.**

Color and Design

It goes without saying that if we choose the right color combinations for our homes, then this will undoubtedly help us create rooms that make us feel good. We all have personal color favorites—you only have to look in someone's wardrobe to discover this. A selection of clothes will be a mixture of instinctive color preferences and what is currently in vogue. When it comes to decorating, however, the stakes are somewhat higher. Mistakes can be expensive and rectifying them can be very time-consuming. So, it makes sense to take time to plan the kind of color scheme you want and how it can be made to work in your home. A lot of this comes down to personal taste again, of course, but, if you do have a grasp of color theory, and know why some colors blend comfortably when they are seen alongside each other, while others seem to vibrate and create visual friction, then you are much more likely to come up with a scheme that really works.

Understanding the color wheel

Color breathes life into a home. It can warm or cool, calm, or excite us. Clever use of color can make small rooms look more spacious or cavernous rooms feel cozy. It can blank out unsightly features and bring the ornate and interesting ones sharply into focus. It has the potential to elevate and enervate all your interior decorating. Never before have home decorators had this much color choice, and the ranges just keep growing—often leading to more confusion and indecision. How can we select colors that are right for us?

COLOR THEORY

Knowing some basic color theory will help you to make color choices that go beyond your gut reaction to a color scheme, although that is also hugely important. Basic color tricks and rules exist, and it is certainly useful to take some time to understand them, even if in the end you decide to break all the rules. Color has always been a tool for self-expression!

Three hundred years have passed since Sir Isaac Newton shone pure white light through a glass prism onto a neutral background and was delighted to see a continuous band of merging color ranging from red through orange, yellow, green, blue, and violet. In essence he had captured a miniature version of the rainbow, which is created by light passing through drops of rain, causing the spectrum colors to be projected like a giant color slide across the sky.

THE COLOR WHEEL

The color wheel is the standard way to explain color mixing by separating the spectrum into twelve different colors. At the center of the wheel is a triangle divided into three equal sections of the primary paint colors— red, yellow, and blue.

These three colors are called primary because they cannot be obtained from a mixture of any other colors. Along with black and white, they form the basis of all other paint colors.

RIGHT **Yellow, red, and blue are the primary colors on which the color wheel is based.**

When colors are arranged as a color wheel, it helps us to understand their relationships to each other and the different effects that are produced when they are used alongside and opposite each other.

Secondary colors are produced by mixing two primary colors:
- yellow + red = orange
- yellow + blue = green
- blue + red = violet.

Tertiary colors are made by mixing a secondary color with an equal amount of the color next to it on the wheel:
- yellow + orange = yellow orange (golden yellow)
- red + orange = red orange (burnt orange)
- yellow + green = yellow green (lime green)
- blue + green = blue green (turquoise)
- blue + violet = blue violet (indigo)
- red + violet = red violet (crimson).

It is also useful to discover how much or how little of one color is added to another to make a third color. Try making your own color wheel.

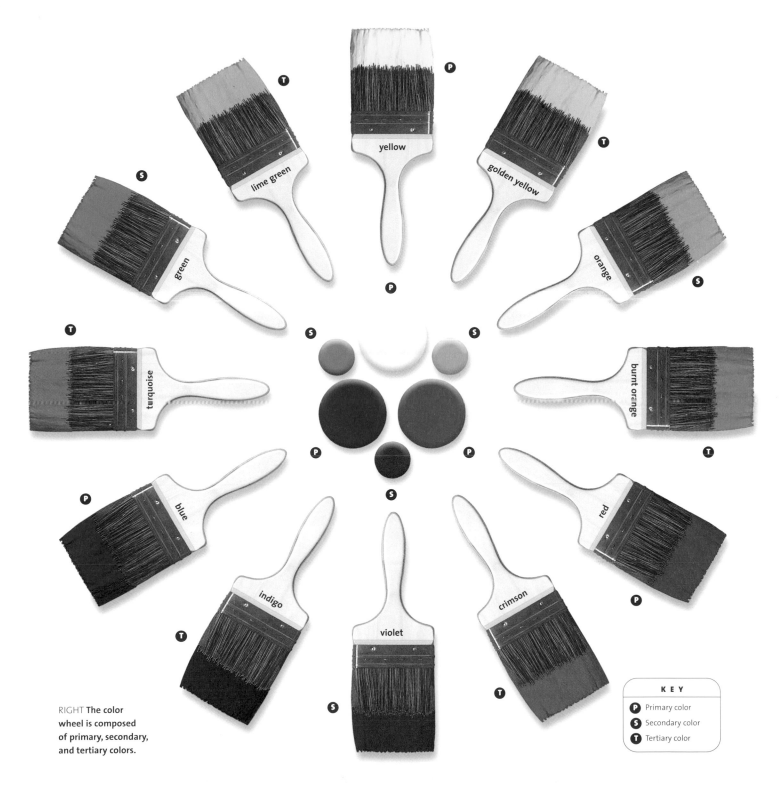

RIGHT **The color wheel is composed of primary, secondary, and tertiary colors.**

KEY

P Primary color
S Secondary color
T Tertiary color

HOW TO MAKE A COLOR WHEEL

1 Begin with a large dab each of primary red, yellow, and blue paint in the middle of a white plate, with yellow at the top, red lower right, and blue in the lower left. These are the **primary** colors and will form the basis of your color wheel.

2 Now mix an equal amount of primary color into the one next to it, around the outside of the original three colors. You will produce orange, green, and violet. These **secondary** colors fill the spaces midway between each two primaries.

3 Place a dot of each primary color on the plate rim opposite its central position, and do the same with the secondary colors. Leave a space between each large enough for the **tertiary** colors (made by mixing a secondary color with an equal amount of the color next to it on the wheel).

Color terms

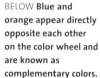 The language used to describe color includes some specific terms that you may not have come across before unless you have studied art or interior design. The few terms that are explained here are those that are most likely to be mentioned within the context of home decorating. Some specialized terminology will come in handy and make it much easier to communicate your thoughts and ideas about color when dealing with professionals in the industry.

LEFT **Golden yellow and mauve clash with each other, producing a kind of visual discomfort.**

BELOW **Blue and orange appear directly opposite each other on the color wheel and are known as complementary colors.**

ADDITIVE COLOR

This is the color of light, where adding all the colors together creates white light.

CLASHES OR DISCORDS

This describes two colors of equal intensity, which cause visual discomfort. Think of them as musical harmonies and discords. Designers and artists sometimes make use of this effect to create a disturbance and give the color scheme an "edge," and color clashes were most famously used in the rebellious 1960s—bright orange and shocking pink, for instance, or golden yellow and mauve.

COMPLEMENTARY COLORS

Colors opposite each other on the color wheel are called "complementary." These are colors of equal intensity. When they are combined in equal proportions they make a neutral gray. When placed alongside each other, they achieve maximum intensity and compete for attention.

ABOVE **In the black and white half of this picture the light foreground and dark background are very clearly defined. In the colored half the tonal contrasts are not as obvious because the glow from the bright yellow illuminates the wall.**

CONTRASTS

Hue

The simplest contrast to understand is that of hue, which describes the difference between undiluted colors seen alongside each other. The primary colors (yellow, red, and blue) are the most extreme example.

Hot and cold

Some colors are hot—red, yellow, and orange; some are cold—blue, green, and violet. The most extreme hot/cold contrasts are red-orange and blue-green.

Light and dark

Light and dark contrast is clear when you look at a color and a black-and-white version of the same photograph. Red and green have the same tonal quality and show up as an equal gray. Yellow and violet are the most extreme examples of this contrast (apart from black and white, which are not colors, but tones).

HUE

A hue is one of the pure colors of the spectrum, like red or yellow, and it can be used to describe the character of another color—for example, lavender has a violet hue, olive has a green hue, or pink has a red hue.

HARMONIES

A harmony is a combination of colors that lets the eye travel smoothly between them with no sharp contrasts. Colors that are close to each other on the color wheel will naturally harmonize—the colors yellow, orange, and red, for example.

INTENSITY

This describes how much pigment is in the paint. The more pigment there is, the stronger and less diluted the color will be. Another word used to describe color intensity is saturation.

NEUTRALS

These are black, white, gray, beige, and cream.

SURFACE COLOR OR PAINT COLOR

This is color that is mixed from pigments, where adding all the primary colors together creates black. This is the color we deal with when decorating, which differs from the colors of light. When all the primary colors of light are combined, the resulting light is white.

TINTS AND SHADES

The addition of white to a color produces a tint, which we call a pastel color; and black darkens a color to produce a shade.

ABOVE **These three blocks are an example of subtle tints and shades. The central color has been lightened by tinting with white (left) and darkened by adding a small amount of black (right).**

Personal taste

If you were to start with a clean slate and were able to reinvent your personal taste, the result is likely to be as sterile as a hotel room or a room set in a furniture show room. These rooms, designed to make many different people feel at home, always lack the character of personal expression. Taste evolves with us, whether as a result of rejecting our parents' taste, or being strongly influenced by fashion or a particular era's decorating style. Our taste in colors also builds up over the years and is developed from an accumulation of influences that go back to childhood.

A BACKGROUND TO YOUR LIFE

Visualize a living room with a white ceiling, pale blue walls, white woodwork, and natural polished wood flooring. This is a traditional classic color scheme, chosen to provide an unobtrusive background for elegant furniture—perhaps some antiques and paintings, and a chandelier. Now place your own furniture in the room and imagine how it will look.

Picture the same room with the baseboards and window frames painted a deep turquoise blue and the walls sunshine yellow. Is this more your sort of look? This is an extreme version of a very useful exercise, because the things you already own and love can provide the best clues when you are looking for a new color scheme.

The front door makes the first statement about who lives behind it, and your color choice can advertise or conceal your personality. Vivid orange, bright golden yellow, or scarlet announce flamboyance and sociability; and deep green suggests a much calmer welcome.

Busy rooms—like family kitchens, where there is a constant flow of traffic and activity—benefit from bold colors and strong contrasts, which add to the room's dynamism. Hallways look inviting in warm yellow or burnt orange, whereas a bedroom is more relaxing if painted a calming green, meditative blue, or lilac.

The way your house functions is improved by the colors chosen for rooms and connecting areas.

LEFT **The detail of this fine old chair would be lost if set against a bright patterned wallpaper. Design your color schemes to flatter the furniture or objects you already own.**

RIGHT **This rough distressed wall finish is a perfect background for a contemporary folding chair. The different textures create a contradiction that gives the image energy. The very old and very new often make good companions.**

Art Deco

In the 1920s the Art Deco style was one of symmetry, stepped shapes, vertical lines, and smooth surfaces. The style was influenced by the Cubist art movement and the arrival of the movies and the great ocean liners. Chrome, glass, ceramics, marble, and leather were some of the most popular ingredients. This was an era when "having style" was considered a top priority. This room features a classic 1920s fireplace and a stunning circular ceiling.

COLOR KEY

1. Cream
2. Plaster pink
3. Warm orange

Diner-style

The 1950s style is bold and fun. In the 1950s, decorating celebrated the return of color after the drab war years, and many of the innovations that had focused on the military were at the disposal of designers for the home market. The plastics industry celebrated with colored laminated surfaces and molded plastic shapes. Chrome kitchen appliances echoed the shapes of streamlined cars and planes and black and white checked patterns added style.

COLOR KEY

1. Ketchup red
2. Gloss white
3. Black

FAVORITISM

We all favor certain colors, and consequently no amount of theoretical knowledge is going to convince someone to paint a room purple if they are of a pastel pink persuasion.

Vive la différence! Each of us is unique, and personal taste varies enormously.

FOLLOWING FASHION

Decorating has always followed fashion. Fashions used to be dictated by kings and queens and ignored at your peril. Scarcity of certain pigments played a large part in how and where they were used, until the Victorians invented synthetic color dyes. Initially pigments were made from earth, minerals, or plants; some were rare and expensive. Blue and purple are two colors whose rarity ensured that they were reserved for royalty and deity, and they still hold these associations today.

These days we are more likely to be influenced by top fashion designers, whose work often encompasses interiors and home accessories. This cross-over has introduced an aspirational feeling to interior decorating and spawned many magazines. Fashion is fun and, because it is ever-changing, it is also refreshing. The latest color scheme can certainly bring a drab room right up to date, but it is important to avoid being a fashion victim. Decorating is big business—to keep the tills ringing, paint companies also ring the color changes every season. But stick to what you like and what suits your room—unless you feel like a change!

Pattern and texture

A colorful room without textural contrasts would look strangely sterile. The texture of an object is one of our key descriptive tools, and a surface pattern can be used to enhance a shape or carry a color scheme. When solid color seems heavy and overpowering over large areas, a patterned version can give a much lighter feel. The dense texture of a carpet means a plain color often works well on the floor but would look better in a sheer version for drapes or a patterned wallpaper.

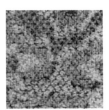
Faux linen: denim blue is a good color for upholstery.

Faux snakeskin: chenille printed in a python pattern.

Woven chenille: a flat weave fabric with a very soft texture.

Woven check: in harmonious orange, yellow, and cream.

Cotton/linen: embodying the English country-house style.

Casbah: this pattern motif works well with a traditional style.

Jacquard weave: a hard-wearing fabric good for upholstery.

Leather: the most hard-wearing of all upholstery material.

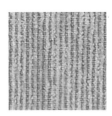
Gold chenille: a rich loose-weave chenille with a corded texture.

Woven dobby: fabric that has the look of brushed denim.

Suède fabric: the look of real suède and a smooth texture.

PATTERN

Interior decorating styles follow catwalk fashions, and most of the top clothes designers now also have home ranges that include furniture, carpets, fabrics, and paint colors. So it is possible to coordinate every area of your life in the style of someone with impeccable design credentials! In real life, few of us would go that far— but it is useful to keep an eye on fashion, where you will find clues to new color trends. Pattern has been kept to a minimum for a long time, but that is about to change, and this is good for home decorators. Pattern is a great way of introducing more color into a room.

TEXTURE

The texture of a color can change its appearance more than you would imagine. Some colors look bland and dead when painted in a mat latex paint. Terra cotta is a good example of this, as it only comes to life on a rough rustic surface or when used as a patchy colorwash. Mint green is another example—it looks fresh and fantastic in a chalky finish, but safe and dull in a flat latex paint. Some colors benefit from having a reflective sheen, especially in combination with a contrasting mat color. Mat chocolate-brown woodwork with a glossy cream wall looks really delicious, and red always looks better with a sheen. The deep green of glass bottles is stunning with light shining through it, but the color is nothing without transparency and light. Experiment with sample pots if you are unsure about which texture of paint will give the look you're after.

A room style based on a natural palette where there is little color variation is brought to life by different textures, such as woven wool, linens, and cottons, sisal matting, sheepskin, leather, bleached wood, and glass. A very little color will go a long way when a rich variety of textures provides the visual interest.

ABOVE **In this room the chalky texture of the walls has been emphasized by the use of a high sheen paint for the chair rail. Chalk finish paints dry to a paler version of the applied color and have a soft, powdery surface bloom. Any type of paint can be given a glossy finish by applying a coat of clear gloss varnish.**

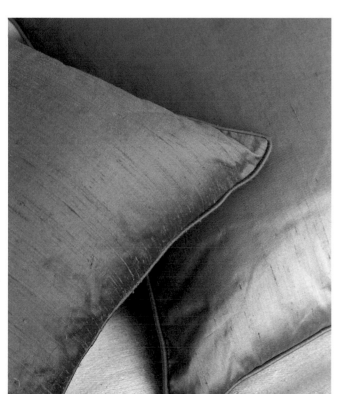

LEFT **Cushions are the easiest way to introduce different textures and colors to a room. Look for cushion fabrics with an obviously contrasting texture to the furniture upholstery, such as these shiny Shantung silks against the unbleached rough linen of the sofa.**

Creating an illusion

Color can be a magical tool if you have awkwardly proportioned rooms, as often happens when houses are converted into apartments. When big rooms are divided up, high ceilings can make them look smaller than they are. This is where clever use of color is useful.

If a room has unusual proportions, color is the cheapest way to improve it without structural alterations. Light colors reflect the most light, making rooms appear bigger and brighter, while dark colors have the opposite effect.

TRICKS OF THE TRADE

A very high ceiling can be made to look a lot lower if a light color is used on the walls up to the height where the ceiling would be in proportion with the room, then a dark color is used above it for the top part of the walls and the ceiling. Fix a chandelier to hang into the room below the dark top section and the high ceiling will "appear to disappear." If you prefer not to have a central light, then make a feature of the lighting by using sculptural contemporary lights to create focal points where you choose to have them, or large table lamps that shed pools of light to give a cozy atmosphere. Look out for the new rechargeable colored balls of light—the charge lasts about four hours, and nobody will ever notice your high ceiling!

A low ceiling will look higher if the walls are painted in a dark color or papered with a "busy" patterned paper up to chair rail height, then painted a very light color above it, including the ceiling. Lighting and color can help exaggerate the illusion of space. Harness blue's receding quality and use subtle washes of light from uplighters to add the most height, like looking up into a pale summer sky. For a fantastic contemporary design solution, try soft washes of slowly changing colored light on a white ceiling to turn your low ceiling into an art feature. Specialized lighting stores have the necessary equipment, and they are a lot less rare than they used to be.

ABOVE **Faced with a room with fine proportions like this one, it would have been a pity to spoil the symmetry by boxing in pipework. The far more sympathetic and successful alternative was simply to paint the pipes to match the background. This works particularly well with a mat paint finish because the shapes don't catch the light.**

LEFT **One way to create a harmonious home is to link the colors of one room with the corridor, stairway, or a feature in the next room. Here the staircase is painted to match the woodwork in the foreground and a band of the blue along the top of the baseboard or string echoes the room's wall color.**

OPTICAL ILLUSIONS

• If the room is long and narrow, it can be made to look wider by painting the longer walls with a cool pale green or blue, so that the walls appear to recede. The narrower walls will appear to advance if you paint them in a deep, warm shade of red or red-brown.

• Paint corridors to harmonize with the room color and remove doors to create a more open-plan sense of space in a small flat.

• Make "small" a virtue by painting walls and ceilings of tiny rooms in deep warm colors for a warming wrap-around coziness.

• Blot out unwanted details like pipework or damaged plaster features by painting them the same color as the surroundings.

• Add interest to a square plain room by creating optical illusions with blocks of color. Drop-shadows, stripes, or stenciled moldings can all be used in contemporary or traditional ways.

ABOVE **You can make a low ceiling seem higher by painting the walls in a dark color and the ceiling in a pale color or white.**

RIGHT **Painting the ceiling in a darker color than the walls of a room will appear to reduce the height of the room and provide a more intimate atmosphere.**

Color and light

The appearance of a color depends on the quality of the light it is seen in. Most of us share the experience of being unable to tell navy blue from black inside a store but once outside the blueness is revealed by daylight. Every color can be enhanced, softened, or highlighted with lighting. The combination of a warm color scheme and soft lighting can create a relaxing environment, and cool colors with sharp contrasts and bright directional light can give a dull space an energetic uplift.

GETTING THE LIGHTING RIGHT

The boldest or most subtle color scheme in the world looks the same in the dark—so it follows that getting the lighting right is absolutely vital. This means making the most of the natural light as well as using the best sort of artificial light for the effect you are after. Anyone who has visited a night club during the day will understand the magic of clever lighting, as daylight reveals what the lighting conceals. If your living room is the children's playroom during the day, then clever lighting tricks can help to create a more sensual atmosphere in the evening. Dimmer switches, uplighters, and concealed lights will create soft ambient lighting conditions, and table lamps make pools of light that add intimacy to a room. Task spotlights can be used for "work" areas such as hi-fi, TV, and games consuls. Use small spots to accent flowers, art, or any other features.

ABOVE, LEFT **Sunlight streams in through the gap between the muslin drapes and the window frame. The muslin softens the light that would otherwise dazzle in a white room. The floor is painted concrete and the walls whitewashed plaster yet the room has atmosphere created by the combination of a cotton rug, an attractive chair, and the quality of the light.**

LEFT **Concealed neon tubes below the wall units illuminate this cool modern kitchen. Kitchens are often too bright but here the task lighting is concentrated on the work surfaces. The light bounces off the one emerald green wall, casting a cool, watery, green light on the whole room.**

LEFT **Rich red walls and a dark rug surround this dining table. The spotlights are all focused on the tabletop, throwing the rest of the room into shadow and creating a sense of intimacy for an adult meal. The high chair in the background gives a hint that this room adopts a very different character during the day.**

BELOW **Yellow is the lightest and the brightest of the primary colors. It glows with reflected natural light and infuses the room with sunshine and warmth. The use of pink in the room beyond has an enticing effect when framed by the yellow.**

A cool, north-facing room can be infused with warmth and light if you paint the walls warm light yellow, and any room will look lighter if you paint walls opposite the windows white or any other very light color. If the windows are small, the natural light in the room will appear to double if the frame, recess, and immediate surround are painted white.

Colored glass or sheets of adhesive color film applied to windows can change the room color during the day. A white room can glow with pink, yellow, or green when the sun shines through the glass, only to return to white again when the sun passes. In the same way, colored lights can be used at night to change the mood and color of a room. One London hotel has a range of colored lighting options in every room, so guests can choose the room's color mood.

Planning color schemes

The starting point here is inspiration, and this could come from a room style seen in a magazine, a classic period style such as Regency, or the regional colors seen on a vacation overseas. Or it could be a combination of colors on a piece of fabric, in the corner of a painting, in a bunch of flowers, or in a bowl of fruit or sugared almonds—anything at all that pleases your eye and could be translated into colors for a room. Analyze the source of your inspiration to discover which of the colors will create the right mood.

SELECTION FACTORS

If the walls are to be all one color, then it should work in context with all the above considerations. Lighter and darker versions of the same color may be a better option, allowing some areas to appear more prominent than others.

Patterned wallpaper could also be used to add texture and variety without introducing another main color. Bold patterns are back in fashion, and the right ones will certainly bring a room right up to date.

If you decide to base your color scheme on an historical or regional style, the color choices will be restricted to particular palettes. The colors simply have to be combined in the traditional way, and success is assured. Everything does not have to be innovative and original, and with color schemes it is generally better to look at something that works well, then copy it.

Decide upon the main colors for the room. The walls, the ceiling, the floor, and the woodwork are the key areas. Unless you are looking to create the illusion of a lower ceiling, then this should be the lightest color in the room. The wall color or colors can be either mat or have a slight sheen. The reflective sheen is best for pale colors where you want to increase the light in a room. Mat gives the most sophisticated look. Gloss is an unusual choice for walls but it is practical for hallways and stairways, especially when there are children in the house.

ABOVE **This rustic Mediterranean home is furnished with an eclectic mixture of art and country furniture. The room is whitewashed and the beams have been picked out in the brilliant blue typical of the region. Blue and white predominate for walls and woodwork, but the bright furnishings, pictures, and flowers create a much more multicolored look.**

features exist does not mean that they have to be picked out and contrasted with the wall color.

Sometimes in a small room a more spacious, expansive effect is achieved by simply painting them the same color as the walls, using a semigloss or satinwood paint. A large room, however, may benefit from the unifying effect of strong bands of color at baseboard, chair, and picture rail height.

FLOORING

A new wooden floor will give any room a very clean, contemporary look, and the cost need not be exorbitant if you choose one of the cheaper laminates. It will provide a good base for colorful rugs, and the "click" type of floorboards do not require glue and can be easily lifted and relaid elsewhere. If existing wooden floorboards are in reasonable condition, they can be painted or stripped and stained. This style of flooring is popular at the moment, and it can always be carpeted over in the future, so there is nothing to lose.

If new flooring is not an option, then the color scheme will have to be chosen to take the existing flooring into account. If you have a rust-colored carpet, for instance, choosing a contrast color like light turquoise or ice blue for the walls will give you a much fresher, livelier effect than a more conventional harmonious yellow, cream, or orange.

PATTERNS

If you would like to use a pattern, there are a few basic rules worth considering. Large patterns work best in large areas and small patterns are best suited to small areas where they can be appreciated. A small floral pattern will read as a texture from a distance, whereas a large floral repeat in a small area is far too overwhelming.

Geometric patterns have recently made a big comeback and, as an alternative to hanging wallpaper, a wall can be treated as a giant painter's canvas with stripes, circles, and squares of color.

ABOVE **Inspiration for planning your color scheme can come from a wide variety of sources in your environment; make a collection of inspiring objects.**

WINDOW FRAMES

Window frames are conventionally painted in a lighter color than walls, as this reflects more light into the room. Unless they are an attractive key feature in the room, such as lovely old double-hung or huge plate glass windows, the frames look better when kept light and neutral, as color will make a feature of any defects.

BASEBOARDS AND CHAIR RAILS

Baseboards and chair or picture rails in older houses provide an opportunity for horizontal bands of color to divide the walls in clean lines. Just because these

Making a swatch board

Not only is this a useful exercise, but it is also great fun. It will help you to make the right choices if you are dealing with something tangible. Begin with your source of inspiration, whether this is a scrap of fabric, a postcard, or a photograph you took on vacation. Place this on a white background to isolate the colors. Take it with you to the paint store, and collect sample paint swatches that match, harmonize, or contrast with it. Look at several different manufacturers' ranges as the colors vary a lot.

ABOVE **This is a swatch board created for a long sunny sitting room with a dining area at one end. The two main colors were used to homogenize the space, and differences in texture defined the areas. A detailed swatch board like this makes it easier to visualize the finished room.**

PAINTED SWATCHES

If your budget stretches to it, then also look at specialist ranges where the colors and finishes are often more unusual. Look out for painted swatches, which are far more accurate than the printed versions. If you are sensitive to chemicals, or simply wish to follow an environmentally kinder route, then send away for the "greener" paint companies' color cards.

Once you have found your colors, buy sample pots and paint them onto a piece of white board (at least 12in sq./300mm sq.) so you can see what the color looks like, and whether it is true to the color card. Placing the board opposite the window, and in a dark corner, will help you judge whether you could go lighter or darker without changing the color. See what it looks like with things you will not change in the room.

Take the color swatch with you when choosing fabric, wallpaper, and carpets. Get samples of anything you like and put them together on the swatchboard. Once you have carpet, fabric, and wallpaper, you will be able to see how the textures affect the colors. Refer back to your original inspiration and compare the colors to the ones that inspired you in the first place. If you haven't managed to find the right colors and you have time for more research, keep looking. There are more paint companies out there than you think, and it is usually the smaller, more specialty stores that deal in the desirable, unusual colors.

BRINGING IT ALL TOGETHER

When you have established your basic color scheme (walls, ceiling, flooring, woodwork, soft furnishings), you can experiment with other textures, patterns, and colors for the accessories. It may be that a very muted color scheme needs a vibrant accent of color to set it off, or conversely that a gaudy background cries out for a plain neutral rug or sofa. A newly painted bare room can look unbearably bright until all your possessions are back in place. Walls can be broken up with pictures, lighting, and shelves, and key wall colors can be picked up on small items like vases, picture frames, cushions, and lampshades to create a more unified color scheme.

ABOVE A beautiful room, which demonstrates successful use of color in interior design. The walls are painted a warm yellow-green, and the same shade appears in the landscape painting. The pictures are thoughtfully hung along a level base line. The natural yellow pine floor is polished to a high sheen to reflect and enhance the natural light, and the rug frames the sleeping area. The simple off-white grid pattern of the rug diffuses the intense indigo blue, creating another level of low-key pattern and color interest. The bed linen in a contrast of muted gray/white stripe and hot salmon pink creates a seductive focal point. The spiky bulrushes and the contemporary black lamp perfectly balance each other's shapes. The room is a wonderful example of harmony, balance, and style.

Textures and Effects

The appearance of color can be completely changed by the introduction of texture. Texture can add depth to a decorating scheme and enhance the impact of different colors. Up until now—and the recent decorating revolution—thick wallpapers and embossed plaster patterns were only used if you had a problem with your walls and wanted to cover it up. An applied texture like this is now seen as a serious design statement, and can add bags of character to a new house or enhance the original features of an older property. You can use different colored and textured paints, natural materials, such as split bamboo, raffia, and linen, and even a cozy fabric like fleece applied directly to the walls. All you need to do is get the colors right, and you're away.

Texture

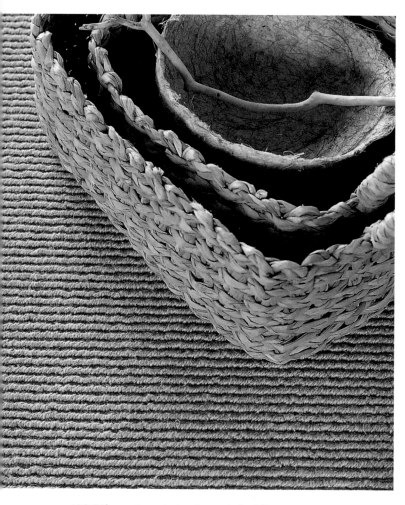

The way we choose and combine different textures for decorating is as much affected by trends as by our color choices. Felt, once used only as a protective barrier, padding or cushioning under a more decorative fabric, now makes a serious fashion statement. Plastic used to be seen as horrible, tacky, and cheap, but now it's the last word in urban chic. Concrete was strictly functional and best kept hidden until minimalists rediscovered its potential. Brightly colored laminated worktops are now back in demand.

ABOVE **The way to use texture in a neutral palette is to set different weaves, stripes, or smooth surfaces against each other. Here we have a corded carpet on the horizontal, with woven baskets on the diagonal to create an energetic textural contrast. The papier-mâché bowl breaks up the pattern and the even smoother stick adds a tactile finishing touch.**

CREATING INTEREST

Texture does not only replace color—it can also be used exclusively for its tactile and visual qualities. The roughness, smoothness, or spikiness of a surface describes its texture. There are endless variations and combinations of textures that can be brought into play to make the home environment a more interesting and stimulating place.

Houses are being built faster than ever these days, with less attention to detail, and wherever we live most of us do it in an arrangement of smooth-sided, interconnecting box shapes. Old houses are more likely to have interesting architectural features to break up the monotony of plain walls, such as plaster moldings, high baseboards, and chair and picture rails. In their absence, there are many wall coverings and specialty paints that can be used to add interest. Anaglypta is a wall texture that has been around for more than a hundred years. The raised patterns were often used in heavy-duty areas such as hallways and staircases, where they adhered with such ferocity that any attempt to remove them brought most of the plaster off the wall as well. The original company still produces textured wall coverings, and has new ranges that look perfect in contemporary rooms. A more recent arrival is a wallpaper range with a raised texture in metallic finishes, which mimics aluminum flooring. It makes the full industrial look much more accessible and less of a permanent commitment, as the surfaces can be painted over with regular latex paint. Other new textures in wallpaper are a mixture of rough and smooth geometric patterns, widely spaced medallion shapes, and ranges of natural materials such as bamboo, linen, or woven reed panels. Cork is another warm, interesting natural texture due for a comeback—it looks good with dark wood, leather, and chrome furniture in sculptural modern shapes, and as a bonus it provides excellent noise insulation.

One of the reasons that the colors we choose from a paint chart surprise us by looking different on our walls is that any variation in texture will introduce elements of light and shade to alter the regularity of the color. Clever use of texture can really add depth to a color scheme, making the difference between an ordinary and an exceptional room.

Our eyes are constantly traveling over surfaces and colors to evaluate and balance what we see. Clever interior designers understand this, and provide interest and relaxation in equal measures, making a room as visually satisfying and comfortable as possible.

ABOVE **This bathroom has an enameled iron bath with bright chrome taps and wood paneling on the walls. The starfish, shells, sponges, and pebbles effectively recreate a sense of the shoreline.**

FAMILIAR TEXTURES

Some of the instantly familiar textures used in the home include: leather • suède • linen • cotton • wool • rattan • paper • rubber • corrugated cardboard • silk • velvet • wood • slate • glass • stone • shell • glazed and unglazed ceramics • cork • marble • PVC • fleece • fake fur • hard plastic • stainless steel • wire mesh • concrete • chrome • rough and smooth wood • foam • feathers • bamboo

LEFT **Green-gray walls with an extreme rustic finish have the potential to look dark and gloomy, but the juxtapostion of a fine wooden table gives a stunningly sophisticated effect. The lilac-glazed ceramic bowl and the high shine of the green apples add two more textures to this very intriguing environment.**

Paint effects

Paint effects have come a long way in recent years—not only do contemporary paint effects look better, but successful application is also a lot easier to achieve. The big paint companies have all produced ranges of special effect products, which are easy to use and guarantee good results. There is a textured paint to make new walls look like those of an old farmhouse. There are shiny, metallic paints that simulate hard metal, and there are even textile finishes to make your walls look like faded denim jeans.

EASY EFFECTS

Paint effects are fun, and there are several that require no specialized training.

WOODGRAINING AND DRAGGING

Essentially woodgraining and dragging are the same kinds of effect; they are both created by dragging a dry paint brush through an oil-based glaze in the direction of the woodgrain. The difference is that in woodgraining you can create effects beyond that of imitating the pattern of the grain.

STENCILING AND SPONGING

It comes as no surprise that stenciling is staging a comeback, because it is the easiest and least expensive way of applying a pattern. Everyone can cut a simple stencil, and there are thousands of more complex designs on the market. Stenciling is something most of us tackle as children but feel wary of trying on the walls. The first secret of stenciling success is using a removable spray adhesive on the back of the stencil so that it sticks to the wall as you paint. The second one is to dip your

ABOVE, LEFT **Woodgraining: you can use a graining comb to make attractive patterns by dragging the comb through an oil-based glaze.**

LEFT **A denim effect wall finish is a soft blue finish available in kit form. The wall is first coated in a pale blue, then rollered over in a denim blue glaze, which is dragged with a long-haired brush.**

RIGHT **Stencil cutting is easier if you stick the pattern onto the card or plastic with a removable spray. Use a very sharp craft knife, inserting the point and cutting away from any corners. Protect the work surface with a cutting mat or cardboard.**

BELOW **Sponging can be done with a natural sponge and paint should be applied quite sparingly. Here a contrasting color is used to demonstrate the technique and a subtler effect can be achieved with a softer combination of colors. Rotate the sponge as you work to avoid a repetitious pattern.**

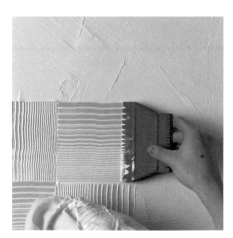

ABOVE **Use a comb or piece of plastic cut to size to create a pattern. This can simply be directional or geometric as here, with one square vertical one horizontal, or you could design your own effect.**

RIGHT **A sponge dabbed onto a textured base will create a simple raised pattern. This can look good in a rustic-style room, and can also be repainted with a foam roller.**

FAR RIGHT **Roll a set of vertical stripes onto the wall from bottom to top and then paint a set of horizontal stripes in another color with a roller to create this plaid effect.**

brush in the paint, then wipe it on paper towels to remove all the moist paint and just leave a dry coating of color. You can always apply more color, but too much will cause blobbing and runs. The same rule applies to sponging, when paint should be applied with a light touch. The textured finishes are applied as a thick coating of plaster-based paint, which is then worked on with a brush, comb, or sponge to score into the surface and lift some of the coating.

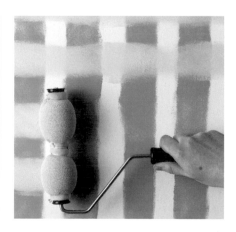

Shades of white

COLOR PALETTE

White comes in a great many subtle variations of color and tone. Just one white standing alone is easily described. It is simply—white. A selection of whites seen together reveal that tones of white can be warm, cool, dull, bright, old, faded, blue, brown, and many more possibilities besides. Brilliant white is the most reflective of all of the whites, and can be hard and dazzling when compared with a color such as bone white, which is warm, soft, and natural, or blue white, which is fresh and cool.

The many white variations that we can now buy as named paint colors have been created to meet the demand for color-free decorating schemes based on the idea of a "pure" style. Color and synthetics have no place in this white world, only natural fabrics and materials in a variety of white textures used together to create a harmonious, peaceful environment. The only acceptable color here is the natural wood used for furniture and flooring, or the living green leaves of an indoor plant. It may sound like an impossible dream, but if the style is used in just one room, it is simplicity itself. A bedroom or bathroom will be easiest, but good storage is essential because colorful clutter will ruin the effect.

Bedroom sanctuary
Use a chalky white water-based paint for the walls. Floors can be sanded and polished if the wood is pale, otherwise floorboards can be painted white. Scattered sheepskins or white flokati rugs are the perfect way to create islands of warmth on wooden floors, and make the most deliciously soft bedside rugs. Sheer, floaty white curtain panels, white wooden shutters, or natural linen shades are all suitable for windows—much depends upon the aspect and the shape of your windows. Almost any style of furniture, old or new, can be used, so long as all fabrics are natural. A regular bed can be transformed into a four-poster by building a simple wooden frame surround and draping it with white muslin tab-topped curtains.

Bathroom sanctuary
This could be achieved with the most basic home improvement toolkit and skills.

If your bathroom suite is white, then you are already halfway there, and white-painted wood paneling or white tiles and towels are all you need. Textural contrasts will make the room look more interesting—mat for woodwork, gleaming tiles, polished chrome, and folded fluffy towels. Flooring could be a good white marble-effect vinyl, or pale gray and white checks with white cotton-twist rugs. Frosted windows with a slight green tint will add extra freshness to a bathroom, and a pretty voile curtain panel will add a softening touch. If any color is used, stick to the very palest shades of gray, fawn, or aqua.

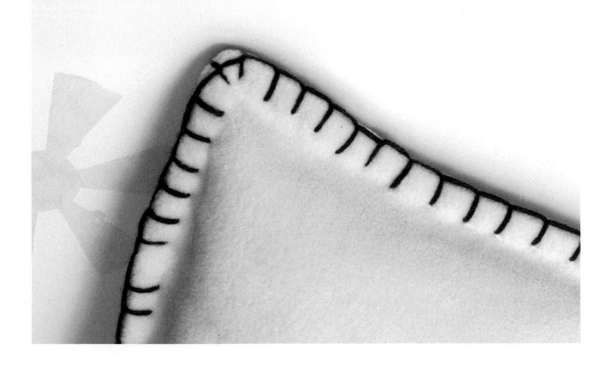

PROJECT
White-on-white stencil effect

COLOR
PALETTE

YOU WILL NEED:

Two shades of white
paint with contrasting
finishes (such as
semigloss and
chalky finish)

Stencil material

A photocopy of
the pattern

Spraymount

Craft knife

Broad stencil brush

Cloth

Plumb line (optional)

Spirit level (optional)

1

2

3

The idea is to stencil a pattern of
contrasting textures, which can either be
rough/smooth, chalky/glossy, or mat/glitter.
The pattern is based on a geometric shape
that is easy to enlarge and cut out. It can
be stenciled in a regular grid pattern, or
used randomly for a more casual effect.

A compromise between the two is best for
large areas, moving a plumb line along a wall
at regular intervals as a guide and stenciling in
a half-drop pattern. Decide on the distance
between the motifs, and stagger the rows so
that in each alternate row the first motif falls
half-way between those in the row before.

COLOR KEY

1 Creamy white

2 Off-white

3 Peach white

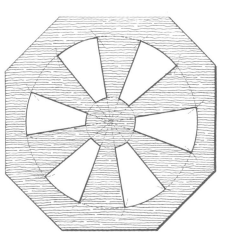

TEMPLATE

This pattern can either be
constructed using a compass and
a ruler or, simpler still, make
a photocopied enlargement of this
diagram to the size of your choice.

HOW TO DO IT

Stenciling a grid of bold shapes on the wall is simple and will give a very contemporary look to any room. To divide a wall into a grid, use a plumb line to mark the verticals and a ruler with a spirit level for the horizontals.

STEP 1 Enlarge the pattern and apply a light drift of Spraymount to the back. Stick it onto a sheet of stencil card or mylar (the clear plastic stencil material).

STEP 2 Cut out the pattern with a craft knife, always cutting away from the corners toward the middle.

STEP 3 Paint the wall with the mat white paint and leave until bone dry.

STEP 4 Spray the back of the stencil with Spraymount and set aside. It should dry to a tacky finish that will stick to the wall when you are stenciling but be easily removed without leaving any sticky residue.

STEP 5 Place the stencil on the wall and use the chalky paint undiluted, applying a generous coating through the stencil with a broad stencil brush.

STEP 6 Lift the stencil and wipe the edges before repositioning it.

Neutrals

The term "neutral" applies to a range of indistinct tones and shades derived from mixtures of black and white with brown, gray, or sometimes with lesser amounts of muddy green, yellow, or blue. A neutral color scheme might be based around soft blue-toned gray or pale khaki brown, but whatever the slight color cast, there will always be a high proportion of white. The neutrals are usually taken from the color of a natural material such as parchment, sand, stone, or marble, and work well with natural textures and materials.

A neutral color scheme does not have to omit color altogether, but the proportion of any other colors used should be small enough so as not to override its basic neutrality. Pattern is one way that a color can be used without overpowering a scheme intended to be seen as neutral. This will work particularly well if the pattern combines the predominant neutral and a color.

A color scheme based around a single neutral does not have to look monotonous if an interesting mixture of tones and textures is used.

Sophisticated beige

A mid-beige vinyl silk paint on walls, with a dead flat darker mushroom beige on all woodwork and an almost white ceiling, does not sound all that thrilling. But add rough woven matting flooring, a large brown and white cowhide rug, loose-weave drapes and a slatted wooden shade, a pale linen-covered sofa with dark beige suède cushions and a mohair throw, and the room has become the epitome of contemporary sophistication. The same theory can be applied to any neutral decorating scheme.

Tranquil haven

A neutral color scheme is superbly restful on the eyes. If you spend your days in an industrial environment or in the heart of a busy city, then this sort of room will be a haven of tranquility at the end of the day. If a room is mainly used in the daytime, a pale neutral scheme will make the most of any natural light, which can be filtered using sheer muslin panels over the windows.

If a room is inclined to feel cold, make your selection from the warmer neutrals with yellowish tones, like cream, sand, and pale straw. They look very good with pale grays or gray-greens. The cooler stone grays can be warmed up by the inclusion of a pinky beige.

Neutral backgrounds may be safe, but they certainly don't have to be dull or boring. A room painted in tones of stone gray on walls, ceiling, and floor is like a vessel waiting to be filled. Strong color statements can be saved for soft furnishings, contemporary furniture, paintings, and dramatic lighting, even flower arrangements. Imagine the gray room with purple floor-length drapes, leather and chrome classic chairs, a red sofa, a row of colored neon tubes, and a giant cactus plant.

PROJECT
Calico drapes

YOU WILL NEED:

Unbleached calico, wide enough for two drapes to cover the window—measure from floor to ceiling and multiply by four (this is to allow for a generous draped heading and some billowing of the drapes onto the floor)

Staple gun and staples

Iron-on bonding tape or double-sided tape for hems

Step ladder

Tie-back hooks

This is a project for those who enjoy a touch of drama with their decorating. It requires no sewing; it can be managed without a pin or a pair of scissors—but you'll need another pair of hands and a stepladder.

It is an unconventional but effective and economical way to drape a large window. The idea is simple enough—to use a single, long length of unbleached calico as two drapes and a draped heading, which is attached to the window frame using a staple gun.

If there is no wooden window frame, a cleat fixed above the window would serve the same purpose.

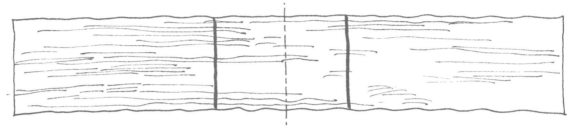

TEMPLATE

Divide the length of fabric in half and mark the center line (above). Measure the window width; transfer the measurement to the fabric, the center line running down the middle. Hold the length of fabric up to the cleat and staple the two corners of the first marked line to the cleat (above). Pleat (see opposite).

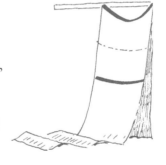 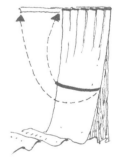

With one side pleated and stapled, pick up the length at the second marked line on the far edge and staple it up to the end of the cleat (above, right). Staple the near edge to meet the first drop. Drapes are tied back during the day.

COLOR KEY
1 Dusky blue
2 Maize
3 Hemp
4 Warm gray

HOW TO DO IT

This is such a stunning window treatment and much easier to do than to explain! It's like riding a bicycle—once learned, never forgotten.

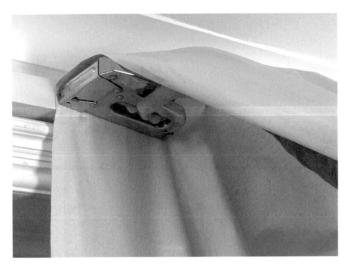

STEP 1 Hem one raw edge, and with a generous amount of this end resting on the floor on the left side of the window, take the rest of the fabric up the ladder with you. Line the fabric up with the top of the window frame and fold it over, letting the excess drop. Staple the fabric to the frame to overlap the center of the window frame by 1in/25mm, then staple the other side to the window frame on the left. Much will depend on the type of window frame, but aim to conceal the top of the frame under the fabric.

STEP 2 If the fabric's width is much greater than half the window, then you will need to pleat the drape. To do this, find the middle and staple it to the middle of the frame. Do the same again on each side of it, and then again, until all the slack is taken up in evenly stapled pleats. Now move the ladder to the other side of the window.

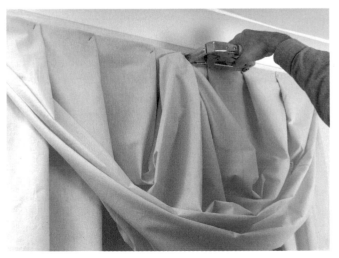

STEP 3 Drape the length of fabric across the top of the window until you reach the right edge of the frame. The line between the corners should fall in a gentle curve (see diagram). Now twist the fabric over, taking the right edge under the drape and into the center, so that the rest of it falls to make the second drape. Staple this right side drape, pleating across the top in the same way as the left side.

STEP 4 Finish off the draped heading by gathering up and stapling the fabric in the middle, so that it falls in even drapes. Make sure that all the staples are concealed by the folds of fabric. Finally, fix tie-back hooks into the sides of the window frame so that the drapes can be gathered up and tied back during the day.

3-D effects with color

COLOR
PALETTE

Color can make a wall shimmer, fade, dazzle, or confuse. The most obvious 3-D effect is produced by using a light/dark contrast to create a drop shadow. This can create illusions such as simple raised panels, recessed niches, or intricate plaster moldings. Colored shapes can be shaded to give them form and the shape of a room can be dramatically changed by the introduction of a false sense of perspective. Once you understand the advancing and receding qualities of different colors, you can produce very convincing effects.

The Ndbele tribeswomen in South Africa paint their simple mud huts externally with architectural features such as columns, pediments, archways, and castellated walls. The background is whitewash, with black outlines and patterns filled in with brilliant colors. It is an idea that can be seen in many parts of the world where paint is used in bold and creative ways to imitate ornate architecture. In Mexico, houses are painted vivid colors with striped bands of contrasting colors. Wall paintings often create 3-D effects and murals are an important part of the local culture and reflect community spirit.

Trompe l'œil

Expert trompe l'œil painters create convincing illusions such as
• walls of shelves stacked with books
• doorways where they don't exist
• windows looking out on panoramic views and many other special effects. Some painters even go so far as to create whole room sets and pastoral scenes on living room and bedroom walls, complete with painted furniture, drawers spilling open to show beautifully painted fabric folds.

There is no need to be that ambitious (unless of course you have the artistic ability!) but there is a lot of fun to be had by using 3-D effects to add life and interest to a featureless room.

In a very plain and box-shaped room, a painted frieze of light and dark geometric shapes can be drawn out with templates. If the angles and the direction of the light are plotted correctly, the effect will be simply stunning and will add a new lease of life to what was previously quite a dull room.

The 3-D project included in this section shows you how to paint blocks of color with dropped shadows. This is a very basic 3-D effect that can be used in a striking way or in a very toned-down way, depending on which room in the house you choose to use it.

It can be a popular choice in living rooms, but it may be best to use small blocks of subtle colors—large blocks of primary colors may prove difficult to live with.

This is a good look in a modern decorating scheme with the minimum of clutter, so there is nothing to take the eye away from the impact of the color blocks.

Go on, dive into the world of 3-D!

PROJECT
Blocks of color with dropped shadow

YOU WILL NEED:

Long rule with
a spirit level

Pencil or chalk

Plumb line

Set square

Painter's tape

Color for blocks

Shadow color

Small roller and tray

Paint brush
(1in/25mm)

This is the simplest three-dimensional effect, whose impact increases with the size of the shapes. The colors chosen for the blocks can be as subtle or bold as you choose. If the room style is based around neutral colors, then using two tones of stone gray will create a subtle paneled effect. On the other hand, primary colors with black shadows on a white background will make the blocks of color appear to leap off the wall. Much depends upon the room's shape, size, and purpose. But beware—a bedazzling optical effect would soon become tiresome in an everyday living room.

COLOR KEY

1 Avocado

2 Red salmon

3 Pure blue

4 Black

HOW TO DO IT

Treat your wall as a blank canvas and create this dramatic effect in the boldest of colors. A 45° set square and a ruler with a straight edge are the essential tools for the job.

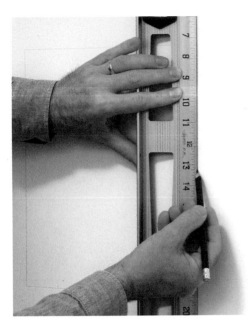

STEP 1 Measure the area and calculate the size and positions of the color blocks. Drop the plumb line to use as a vertical guide and use the long rule to mark out rectangular shapes in pencil.

STEP 2 Place a strip of painter's tape around each of the shapes, then apply the color with the small roller. Leave to dry, then peel off the tape. Leave overnight until bone dry.

STEP 3 Use the set square to draw a shadow box at 45° on one side and the base of each block. Place a strip of painter's tape around the shadow area, including the two inside edges of the color block.

STEP 4 Paint the shadow with the brush and leave the paint to dry before peeling off the tape.

Color Highlights

Attracting attention and maybe distracting the eye from a less deserving area is the general idea of a highlight, and color can be used very effectively in this capacity. Color highlights can also create a more energetic environment, but in order to work they have to be seen against a neutral or tonally similar background—they are no good if the room is already a total riot of color! The secret of color highlighting is that the strongest impact is achieved when the highlight color is used in moderation—too much and it becomes a feature, too little and it can become overlooked. Remember that the highlight does not have to be a strongly saturated color—a flash of pale apricot seen against dark gray would be as effective as violet purple against baby pink.

Adding focus

The process of decorating involves a lot of visualization, preparation, shopping, and plain hard work. The inspiration for a color scheme or room style may have come from something seen in a magazine, on vacation or in someone else's home, but the results are disappointing because, although the general look is the same, something is missing. The room has changed, but with all the hard work completed an extra something is needed to pull the look together. This something is the room's focus.

THE CREATIVE PATH

Most rooms will have some individuality, a feature such as the fireplace, a doorway, a nice floor, or perhaps a style of window that becomes the natural focal point. If nothing is striking enough to become an area of focus, then one can be created with color. This could be done with paint; it could be as simple as painting a contrasting colored shape on one of the walls, or painting blocks of color as broad borders for framed pictures. More often, though, it is done by introducing some new element, which could be a painting, a sculptural piece of furniture, a rug, or a wonderful plant. This does not necessarily mean spending a lot of money. The art could be a row of pebbles in a straight line, a strangely shaped piece of driftwood displayed on a bright background, or a pile of pine cones sprayed shocking pink. A canvas floorcloth can be painted and stenciled for a fraction of the cost of buying a rug, or you could paint a rug directly onto the floor. It is important to enjoy the decorating process, and taking the creative route is always more rewarding than shopping—well, nearly always!

LEFT **This circular rug has radiating colored lines that attract the eye to its color, shape, and size. A bare floor is fine for dancing, but rugs make a room much more homely.**

KEEPING THINGS IN PROPORTION

Proportion is very important, as there is a big difference between attracting attention and dominating a room. An exuberant palm in a ceramic pot looks great—as long as it's not so great as to infringe on your space! In just the same way, something that is far too small in proportion to its surroundings doesn't work either. A small handmade designer rug will still attract attention in the middle of a large open expanse of floor, but it will look mean.

SMART BUT SIMPLE

Choosing wisely does not always mean spending a lot of money. One idea which works very well is repetition. Instead of buying one large vase, buy four in the same style but in different colors, and arrange them in a straight line. This will create a color rhythm and focus, and need not cost very much at all. The same could be done with something completely free, like green-tinged cola bottles, which are design classics. A line of them becomes a sculpture in the right setting.

Fresh flowers are the most reliable way of adding instant focus to a room. Depending on what you choose, flowers can be used to change the mood of the room—they can even be used to reflect your own mood, if you like! For instance, if you're feeling romantic, choose roses; and if you're feeling full of the joys of life and you don't care who knows it, go for lilies. Many flowers come in a whole range of gorgeous colors, so you should have no problem working with your room's color scheme, and changing the atmosphere throughout the year. An arrangement of striking seedheads from the garden can also make a really stunning display.

If a bunch of flowers seems too much of an indulgence, just buy one or two single stems and angle a spotlight their way. This little trick creates a tremendously cool, contemporary effect.

Window treatments

Windows are one of the main focal points in any room because of the light coming in and the view of the outside world that they reveal. Windows also give us an opportunity to introduce color and pattern that will flatter the room's color scheme and pick up on colors used elsewhere in the room. The biggest mistake is to treat the window in isolation without taking the rest of the room into account, because the right window treatment will make any room look a hundred times better.

ABOVE **When a room has a fabulous view, nothing should be allowed to interfere or detract from it. Window frame colors or drapes should create a perfect frame for the view, choosing either a strong contrast as an outline or a harmonious shade to create a more natural progression from room to view. In this room there are no drapes to complicate the scene, and the frames have been painted to match the blue-green of the trees.**

THE RIGHT TREATMENT

There are so many different ways of covering windows, and some solutions will only suit certain situations. Consider whether the room is mainly to be used during the day or at night, what the room's purpose is, and if there are any practical limitations on the type of window treatment that would suit the room. In a room which has direct early morning sunlight, drapes will need black-out linings or blinds; one that is overlooked by other windows will need muslins or nets for privacy, and windows opening onto a busy street will soon make drapes grimy and the chosen fabric will need to be one that will not deteriorate with regular washing.

Sometimes, the view from a window is simply too stunning to conceal—a view of city lights at night, for instance, can be hundred times better than the same view during the day when it would be better obscured by slatted shades, which would also soften and filter the light. A large picture-window view over a garden or fields will be the room's best feature in daylight, but can make the inhabitants feel too exposed after dark, when thick drapes would make the room feel more intimate. Ruling out specific window treatments is helpful as this will help to narrow down the options and let you focus on what will look best.

When in doubt, do something creative and temporary while you decide. If there is a drapery rod, use cotton sheets or saris, draped or with curtain clips.

SUBTLE COORDINATION

The over-coordinated decorating style where the same fabric is used for furnishings and drapes is very dated, and looks as impersonal as a hotel or a furniture showroom. Try picking up a theme instead with, for instance, sari-style fabric used for drapes and embroidered silk cushions in matching colors, making a link between the furniture and the window treatment. A crocheted white lace panel pinned across a window in a simple Mediterranean-style bedroom will echo the lace cloth on a bedside table. A bright orange roller shade will warm up a shaded north-facing window, and something as simple as a bowl of oranges will match the color and balance its brilliance in the room.

ABOVE **Simple roller shades are one of the most economical window treatments and they have the added benefit of obscuring only a small part of the window surface. This means they can be adjusted to let maximum light into a room when needed or pulled down to reveal the pattern and provide privacy in the evening.**

LEFT **It would be a pity to hide a deep window recess like the one in this cottage. The wooden paneling adds to the sense of perspective and creates the perfect frame for the flower arrangement. Painting a deep recess in light gloss paint will bring more light into the room.**

Window treatments

DRAPES AND SHADES

If walls are painted in plain colors, then drapes can be patterned in harmonious or contrasting colors, but when using pattern proportion is very important. As a rule, large patterns need large areas and small patterns work best when they are seen at close range.

Colored transparent fabrics look pale with daylight shining through them, but their color looks stronger in the evening, especially if the windows are fitted with roller shades. Shades are a good way of adding color to a room, and a contemporary-styled room with a row of windows looks good with a different color shade in each one. A shade fitted into the window recess can remain in place if drapes are added, but will also look good on its own.

Roman shades are very easy to make—they hang in folds, and can be made in most fabric weights from heavy canvas to soft voile. They are also the most

economical treatment as they hang as a flat panel to match the dimensions of the window.

When in doubt, choose a plain neutral color and a classic window treatment rather than something wildly fashionable if you are buying a good quality fabric, as this will not date. If you are on a tight budget, look at alternative fabrics, especially from street markets near garment-making districts, for example, unbleached calico, bed sheeting, felt, fleece, or suit linings.

LEFT **This light, harmonious, and thoroughly grown-up living room has been designed around a single shade of lilac. The furniture, woodwork, and soft furnishings all match, and the gingham and plaid check of the drapes prevents the effect from becoming too bland.**

ABOVE **Full-length yellow drapes frame this window, and the sun filters through to cast a warm glow of light into the room. The soft furnishing colors used here are cool, with greens and blues mellowed by the brilliance of the yellow drapes. When drawn, the drapes almost fill the wall, making an even bolder yellow statement.**

LEFT **Floral Roman shades with a dark border are teamed with simple sprigged muslin drapes for these glazed doors. This is a perfect solution for doors that are often in use, as they can be left open to admit the light or closed to provide shade.**

Soft furnishings

Soft furnishings are the fabrics we use in the home to add character and instil our own personalities. As very few of us undertake the making or even reupholstery of sofas, armchairs, or beds, it's the cushions, shawls, throws, lampshades, tablecloths, and bedspreads we add that change something mass-produced into something uniquely ours. The idea is make the room look more attractive and increase the level of comfort, so choose soft fillings and fabrics that are tactile as well as beautiful.

ABOVE **Choose cushions of the same style in different colors to give a harmonious look. These embroidered cushions in purple and olive are exotic and inviting against deep rose chenille upholstery.**

RING THE CHANGES

Soft furnishings can be changed with the seasons, creating a light, airy style in summer and a warm comfort zone for the winter. A sofa can be covered with a fleece throw for winter and cotton for summer. In the days before central heating, this was a normal part of home life, with soft flannel sheets and woolly rugs for winter and crisp cotton sheets and light woven floor mats in summer. Winter drapes were heavy and thick to block out the cold drafts, but summer was a time for net, lace, and cheerful cotton prints. Nostalgia can be fun and there is always room for retro style in fashion.

Color has a huge role to play in soft furnishings, especially if the room is simply decorated in plain colors. A room could be painted off-white with unbleached muslin drapes and chair covers, but still be perceived as colorful if the sofa and chairs were piled with an assortment of vividly colored cushions, the floor boasted a bright patterned dhurrie, and the table lamps had equally vibrant shades. To see how soft furnishings can alter a room's character, first imagine a golden yellow bedroom with an iron bed draped with a rich red velvet bedspread and bolster cushions, then change the bedding to a blue and white striped duvet cover. The whole mood has swung from luxurious and exotic to fresh and breezy. Put the idea into practice by using different fabrics and accessories in your bedroom to spice it up or cool it down to suit the mood.

COLOR COORDINATION

A monochrome color scheme can look bland without the right type of soft furnishings. One solution is to choose a range of patterned fabrics that are not usually seen together, in a single color. This could mean mixing classic patterns such as toile-de-jouy, stripes, tie-dye circles, and floral damask to make a set of unmatched cushions. Keep the rest of the room neutral and leave the cushions to make the color statement. The beauty of this style of color coordinating is that you can usually buy remnants of expensive fabric in amounts sufficient for cushion covers at a fraction of the cost of buying it off the roll. Make it a rule always to have a rummage in remnant bins anyway, and build up a treasure chest of fabric for future soft furnishing projects.

LEFT **Rich, varied textures and weights of fabrics in shades of yellow.**

ABOVE **The secret of creating a Japanese look means taking a no-frills, minimalist approach to both color and design. Cream, red, and black are all the colors you need.**

LEFT **A thick gold and red curtain softens the hard edges of the doorway, and the same colors are picked up in the soft covers of the dining chairs in the background. A band of contrasting color could be used to join short remnants of superior quality fabrics and create a luxurious draped curtain like this one at a bargain price.**

Painted floors

The idea of painting floors is a very old one that has become popular once again. One of the most attractive aspects of floor painting is how inexpensive it is in comparison to other floor treatments. A floor often needs only a light sanding to prepare it and many paint companies have added special floor paints to their product ranges. If you use conventional paint, add a couple of coats of strong polyurethane varnish to keep the color fresh or, for a more lived-in style, just let the wear and tear show through.

PREPARING THE FLOOR

If you are thinking of painting the floor and have first to dispose of carpets or old vinyl, it is wise to have a peep underneath to assess the condition of the floorboards. If the flooring has been stuck to the boards with carpet tape, you will need to use a sander to remove the sticky tape. If the floor would benefit from a good sanding, then it would be best to rent a machine for a day. The sanding machine rental is not hugely expensive but cost of the special sandpaper can add up, so do make it clear in the rental store that you are sanding to prepare for painting rather than to expose the true beauty of the natural wood. Using a sanding machine does not require great effort but it creates a lot of noise and dust and you have first to remove everything from its path. Once the floor has been sanded, it can be wiped over with sugar soap and left to dry before painting.

The most important thing to remember when painting a floor is to begin in the far corner and end in the doorway! A standard paint roller and tray do the job very well unless you are painting the boards different colors, when it is advisable to use a small foam roller or a paintbrush. The paint is best applied in thin coats with adequate drying time between.

Patterned floors can either be stenciled or marked out in chalk and filled in with a paint brush. One of the most timeless painted patterns is a simple checkerboard which can be painted directly onto floorboards or onto sheets of hardboard tacked over the boards if you prefer a smoother 'marble' finish.

There are several ways of painting a checkerboard, which can be done diagonally or horizontally. Painter's tape can be used to outline the squares. It makes painting easier, but mask and paint only a few squares at a time because it can cause confusion and ruin the pattern over a large area. The simplest method is to mark out the floor in pencil or chalk by drawing around a square template. The stark contrast of black and white can be very unforgiving of any wobbly edges, so choose gray, coffee brown, or sage green and off-white instead for a softer but very stylish flooring effect.

SPECIAL FLOOR PAINTS

You can now buy paint made specially for vinyl floors, which means an end to the days of putting up with nasty patterns when you move into a new place, just because the flooring is in too good a condition to justify replacing it. All you need is a pot of paint and a roller to transform a bad floor with a tasteful mat dusky blue, sandy yellow, or barn red. Now that's progress!

There are also specialized paints for concrete floors that give a more finished, homely look. Concrete is a cold indoor flooring material suitable only for warm climates or conservatories. It is popular in the South of France, where stunning patterned floors are created with inlays of beach pebbles.

PROJECT
Painting a floor

YOU WILL NEED:

Primer for bare wood
or undercoat

One color of floor
paint (or use latex
paint with heavy-duty
polyurethane varnish)

A 2in/50mm
household
paint brush

A large roller and tray
for the primer and
varnish if using

Clear heavy-duty
mat or gloss varnish

Painter's tape

Once you have decided to paint a floor, everything will have to be removed from the floor area. Examine the floorboards closely, checking for any protruding nails, which should be banged in using a hammer with a nail punch. Splintered boards must be sanded and any holes filled with a good quality wood filler. Sand the floor lightly, then sweep up all the dust and wash the boards with a sugar soap solution to get rid of any grease. A proper floor paint will give the best finish and last the longest; otherwise, apply two coats of floor quality varnish after the paint.

HOW TO DO IT

Painting a floor in a single color could not be simpler. It does not take long and the effect will be one of instant freshness.

STEP 1 Mask off the baseboards to floor level.

STEP 2 Begin with the brush, painting the primer into the edges of the floor, right into the corners and up to the painter's tape.

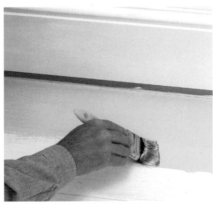

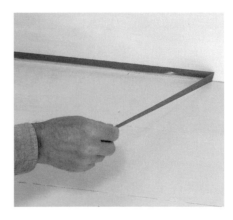

STEP 3 Then apply the primer to the rest of the boards with the roller and leave to dry. Apply the floor paint in exactly the same way. Two thin coats will give a better finish than one thick one.

STEP 4 Leave the paint to dry overnight for the best results. Carefully remove the masking tape from the baseboards.

Creating a Style
With Color

Certain color combinations have become synonymous with particular places—this is due to the rich variety of historical and cultural influences in our world, as well as the differences between urban or rural environments and hot or cool climates. Colors can also evoke very strong memories and associations, and these transport us to faraway places. A holiday postcard can become the basis for a whole new decorating scheme, with chalky white paint and bright blue woodwork reflecting the Greek islands, for example, or faded earthy colors bringing back the essence of elegant Venice. The most important thing when you are planning on recreating the style of anywhere, however, is to get the colors exactly right.

English country

The English country cottage is a very cozy and welcoming place where there are roses and honeysuckle around the door in summer and usually a freshly baked cake for tea. In the winter time there will always be a log fire burning in the grate and a soft wool shawl draped over the back of the sofa for that little bit of extra warmth. If you get the look right, visitors should immediately feel so at home that they flop down in a comfortable chair, put their feet up and ask for a cup of tea. In fact, you may have to use force to evict them!

English country style is eclectic, and only really works well when old and new are mixed together. Aim for the impression that furniture and accessories have been passed down through the family for several generations. If you are starting from scratch, shop around at antique markets, garage sales, and craft fairs. The right framed mirror or china bowl can make all the difference and need not cost a fortune—imperfections, chips, and worn edges actually enhance the look.

Pattern is one of the key ingredients, and many different styles can be successfully combined, including woven woollen plaids, Indian and Turkish rugs, tapestries, plain and floral cotton chintz, damask, and lace.

Old and mellow

Floral patterned fabrics are now produced in soft faded colors, or you could search out genuine vintage fabrics at charity sales or flea markets. One old chintz curtain can make a whole set of plump cushions if you're handy with a sewing machine.

In old country cottages with exposed beams, walls are usually rough plaster painted white, pink, or creamy yellow. Low ceilings and small windows can make rooms dark and gloomy, but by painting window recesses glossy white you can virtually double the amount of incoming natural light. Another trick is to position mirrors opposite windows to reflect the light back into the room.

Faking it

If you don't have a sweet little beamed country cottage, but still want to decorate in the English Country style, the first thing to consider is the proportions of the room. Even the most boxy plain room can be made to look a lot cozier with the right wall treatment, colors, and lighting. Walls can be tongue and groove paneled up to picture rail height with a shelf running above the paneling. Or apply a rough textured paint to give the impression of an uneven surface and rough plasterwork. Stenciling works well on rough surfaces and is perfect in a country setting. Patterns can either be cut at home, taking inspiration from textiles in the room, or bought ready-cut.

The key colors are taken straight from the cottage garden: soft powder blue, cream, all shades of pink, pale, moss and grass green, brown, and brick red.

PROJECT
A rose-stenciled wall

YOU WILL NEED:

Powder blue paint
for background

Sample pots of
two pinks

Sample pot of green

Stencil material
(mylar or stencil card
if you prefer), or buy a
ready-cut rose stencil

Spraymount

Craft knife

3 stencil brushes

3 white saucers

Plumb line

Square of card (to
mark distance
between motifs)

If you like pattern and have uneven walls, then stenciling is the way to go, as wallpaper requires walls that are smooth and even. This is a very romantic, feminine style for a pretty bedroom. The blue rose-patterned walls have a look of faded textiles and combine well with lace, muslin, and plenty of vintage floral fabrics used for cushions and bed covers. The walls provide a perfect backdrop for traditional bedroom furniture like dressing tables, Lloyd loom chairs, iron bedsteads, and closets. Keep a look-out for pretty old vases, mirrors, and lamps that will add authenticity to the look.

COLOR KEY

1 Soft peacock blue

2 Deep rose pink

3 Pale pistachio

4 Rose pink

TEMPLATE

Copy this pattern or enlarge it using the grid system. We used the rose pattern at the size of 2½in/60mm across. The stencil can be cut from waxed card or special stencil plastic available from craft stores.

HOW TO DO IT

Stenciling a wall pattern is quicker than putting up wallpaper and also a lot cheaper. Use the smallest amount of paint on your brush and practice on paper before you tackle the wall.

STEP 1 Make the pattern for the stencil. Coat the back of the pattern with Spraymount and stick it onto the stencil material. Use a sharp craft knife and cut out the stencil carefully.

STEP 2 Peel off the paper pattern, then spray the back of the stencil with Spraymount and leave it to become tacky.

STEP 3 Hang the plumb line 10in/250mm from one corner of the wall and position the card with the line running through two corners. Make a pencil mark at each corner, then move the card down, placing the top point on the lowest mark, and repeat to the baseboard. Mark up the whole wall in this way.

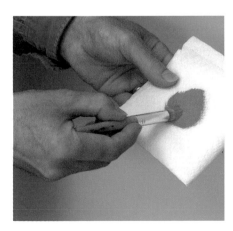

STEP 4 Position the stencil and smooth it onto the wall. Put the paints on the saucers and dab off brushes with paper towels so little remains on the brush.

STEP 5 Begin stenciling with the dark pink in the middle of the rose, then move on to the pale pink for the outer petals. Lift the stencil to check on the result as you go.

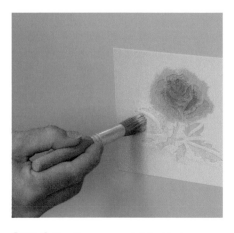

STEP 6 Use the green paint for the leaves and stem. Lift the stencil to check the result. Position it on the next mark and repeat the pattern until the wall is covered with roses.

Pure Romany

Romany style is most suited to people who prefer to keep one foot in the past and whose idea of bliss is a country kitchen with a cooking range. Rich, dark background colors are decorated using the light touch of single freehand brushstrokes, with each pattern being composed of a mixture of stripes, swirls, dots, and curves. Romany inspiration comes from the countryside and nature; flowers are the most popular decorative motif. Red, green, black, and white are the main colors, but many other colors can be used for the decoration.

The colors explode with all the fun of the fair. Bright canal barges, decks piled high with vividly patterned tinware, fairground stalls, and painted gipsy caravans are the inspiration for this look. Painting patterns were handed down through Romany families, and as lifestyles changed, many of the traditional skills have disappeared. Fortunately the lazy, slow, canal-boat lifestyle appealed to people looking for an escape route from the fast pace of modern life, and since the 1970s many canal boats have been restored and brought back to their former vivid beauty. The main patterns used include flowers, leaves, castles, bridges, horses, playing cards, scallops, and striped bands of color. Lettering is often part of the design, spelling out the name of the barge or its owner.

Free style

If the idea of living in a painted horse-drawn caravan or a canal boat sounds appealing but impractical, then why not settle for bringing some of the color and atmosphere into your home? The bright colors are set against a dark background of either black, dark green, or blue, and all the patterns are painted freehand. It is a true peasant painting style, which is great fun to do as it requires the type of loose, confident brush stroke that is best achieved after a glass or two of wine!

If you love the patterns but find the brilliance of the colors too overwhelming, try artificially fading them with a milky glaze of varnish tinted with a small amount of white. This effect will be more like an old sun-bleached painted caravan needing a fresh coat of paint. If this appeals, then you could take the illusion a stage further and rub back some of the paint to simulate wear and tear.

Small is beautiful

On a large scale this would be quite overpowering, but it is perfect for a small cubby-hole of a room, or just as part of a room. This project shows you how to make a pair of vibrantly patterned drapes to hang at your window. This window treatment will look equally good as the focal point in quite a plain room, as one of many patterns in a busy kitchen, or to add a touch of fantasy in a child's playroom. And a painted window-box filled with flowers outside the window is the perfect finishing touch.

PROJECT
Making felt appliqué drapes

① ② ③ ④ ⑤

YOU WILL NEED:

Cotton drill:
2 x double the
window width
x the height plus
100mm/4in

Felt in 4 other colors
(for example, green,
white, black, yellow)

Buttons for
decoration

Thread

Lining fabric—can be
cotton sheeting

Sewing machine

Rufflette tape for
curtain headings

Curtain rings

Fabric glue

A brush

COLOR KEY

1 Leaf green
2 Scarlet
3 Deep sage green
4 Cream
5 Black

Felt decorations can give drapes a stylish, brightly colored Romany look. Felt pattern shapes can be cut out and stuck down with glue. Although felt does not wash well, the colors are bright and will stay fresh-looking for a couple of years. The drapes are backed with a plain cotton lining.

Romany style has always included a variety of textiles—hand-dyed, woven, embroidered, and appliquéed. The main pattern theme is a flower treated in a stylized way. These floral patterns are taken from Eastern European folk art and arranged in a typical way for decorating a long skirt or an apron.

TEMPLATE

Draw these patterns or copy them (enlarged to the desired size) and cut them out of thin paper. Then pin the patterns to felt and cut out the shapes.

HOW TO DO IT

These drapes are lined and headed with a simple tape and curtain rings. The decoration is glued in place with strong fabric glue but could also be fixed in place using a contrasting blanket stitch.

STEP 1 Cut out all the curtain and lining lengths. Draw the pattern shapes and cut them out of the colored felt.

STEP 2 Arrange the pattern shapes on the background, then glue each one in position (if you like hand-sewing, then these can be edged in contrasting running stitch or blanket stitch).

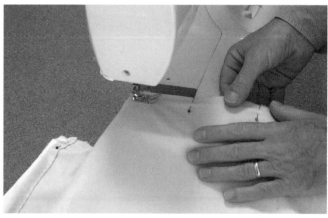

STEP 3 Turn over a narrow hem on the lining side seams, then pin the linings onto the front of the drapes along the top edge, allowing roughly 1in/25mm for the seam. Stitch, then turn the lining over onto the back and press the top seam flat.

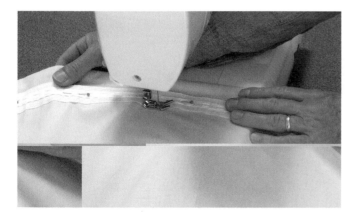

STEP 4 Pin the heading tape to the lining about 1in/25mm from the top edge, then stitch it using the same color thread as the felt drape so that the stitching is invisible on the front.

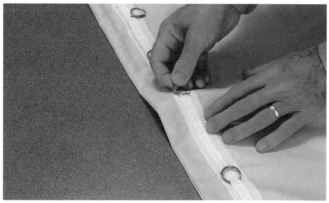

STEP 5 Fit the curtain rings onto the heading tape and hang the drapes from the rail. Pin up the hem with the lining tucked into the seam, then loosely slip-stitch the hem (this can be done without taking the drapes down).

Tuscany

COLOR PALETTE

Tuscany in summer presents the perfect antidote to a gray winter spent in a city—the effect is instantaneous and unforgettable. Italy, like every other industrialized society, has moved away from old-style farming and many Italians choose new, problem-free housing with all mod cons over the tumbledown old farm buildings that fire the visitor's imagination. The restoration of farmhouses and villas in the Tuscan countryside has largely been undertaken by outsiders, for whom it was a case of "love at first sight."

It seems that another culture's rural lifestyle always has more appeal than one's own, doubly so when the weather is good. The outsiders have rescued what the locals would have thrown out in the name of progress, and craftsmen have found their traditional skills in great demand.

Tuscany has a treasury of art, architecture, and culture in cities such as Florence and Siena, where the climate has helped to preserve its beauty. The colors of marble, earth, and clay predominate, with the sun playing its part by fading fresh paint to blend seamlessly with the colors of older buildings.

The Tuscan climate is hot and dry, and houses are built of local stone with curved earthenware roof tiles. Windows have wooden shutters and the coloring of the buildings lets them blend into the landscape.

Simple and functional

Inside, the houses have tiled floors and plastered walls painted in pink, shades of faded blue green, or ocher yellow. There are no baseboards, but the lower part of the walls are painted in a darker color to hide the scuff marks made by the broom.

The small windows shield interiors from the scorching heat of the summer sun and the cold winter nights. Drapes are rare, but wooden shutters are fitted inside the windows, making it easy to block out the light during the afternoon rest hours. Window ledges are tiled, and the broad bands surrounding windows and doorways are picked out in softly contrasting colors. The paint used in Tuscany is always limewash tinted with pigments. This is the perfect paint for the climate, and the chalky finish is essential for the authentic Tuscan look.

The furnishing style is simple and functional, as most entertaining takes place outside on the terrace. In Italy, furniture is often arranged against the walls rather than in the center of a room to keep an open, spacious feeling. A few pieces of wooden furniture, some hand-painted ceramics, pot plants, Turkish rugs, and table lamps are all in keeping with this style. Terra cotta floor tiles are practical in an entrance hall and a kitchen, but are only suitable for living rooms in warmer climates. Polished floorboards and rugs look good and feel warmer underfoot.

The key to success is to keep it simple.

PROJECT
A painted wall finish

COLOR
PALETTE

YOU WILL NEED:

Three shades of
chalk-finish paint

Large paint
brush suitable for
color-washing

Paint kettle

Painter's tape

Long rule with
spirit level

Pencil for marking
the wall

The Tuscan decorating style is a simple one that uses weathered, textured, and harmonious color with no hard lines, startling primary colors, or sharp contrasts. The look is not difficult to reproduce with Mediterranean paint that dries to a chalky finish. A slightly textured wall surface and color-washed effect will intensify the Tuscan flavor, and the rough texture can be effectively applied with a special textured paint in a sand or farmhouse finish. The color here is also used to surround the small key cabinet to add to the illusion of it being a shuttered window.

COLOR KEY

1 Deep ocher
2 Dark terra cotta
3 Deep purple

HOW TO DO IT

Keep the brush strokes fresh and energetic and use chalky water-based paint for an authentic Tuscan wall finish.

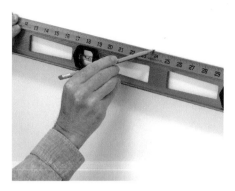

STEP 2 Measure 3ft/1m up from the floor and mark the wall at intervals. Draw a line along the length of the wall.

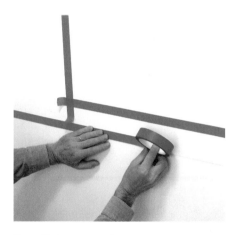

STEP 3 Place painter's tape on the lower side of the 3ft/1m line and inside the border line.

STEP 1 Measure a border of 4in/100mm around any window, doorway, or fitted feature, such as a cabinet, and mark this in pencil.

STEP 4 Dilute the paint and apply it to the lower wall and inside the inner border for the feature using random brush strokes. Then leave it to dry.

STEP 5 Renew the tape and paint the top part of the wall and the outer border of the feature using the second, diluted paint. Peel off the tape and paint a freehand stripe in terra cotta across the wall.

Moorish casbah

The Moorish style comes from the north of Africa where Morocco nestles between the Atlas mountains and the sea. This meeting point of African and Muslim culture has a rich artistic and cultural tradition. Islamic art and decoration is based on geometric patterns as the religion forbids the making of images. Houses are built around inner courtyards with plain, fortress-style exteriors; all of the decoration is on the inside. The courtyards are lined with open balconies, often with rows of columns and elaborate arches.

One of the most stunning features in Moorish homes is the tiling. Tiles are used on walls and floors to create elaborate interwoven shapes and patterns. The star features in most patterns, usually in the center of a radiating trellis-work of star patterns. The main colors used are blue, white, black, pale green, and terra cotta. Colors are jewel-bright, whether on walls, tiles, or woven in textiles.

Domes and arches

Other important features in Moorish design are domes, arches, and water. Doorways are arched and windows are usually covered with decorative metal grilles. Walled rooftop terraces are the most popular place for evening entertaining. Walls are either topped off with stepped patterns or simply castellated and whitewashed to reflect the searing heat. Pools and fountains cool the courtyards, and date palms provide shade.

Pierced lanterns, leather pouffes, carved tea tables, and intricately woven rugs are typical furnishings. Low couches are spread with rugs and silk cushions in all shapes and sizes. It is a style that encourages relaxation and a more exotic, sensual way of living.

Moroccan style is not expensive or beyond our reach thanks to the market culture which exists at the source in Morocco and in all major cities in Europe. The hippy trail led straight to Marrakesh in the late 1960s, and people soon discovered that they could finance their nomadic lifestyles by buying Moroccan goods and selling them back home to fund their next visit. As a result, the markets were flooded with folding tables, rugs, lanterns, trays, and ceramics, many of which can still be picked up at reasonable prices in flea markets today. The ethnic decorating style which has been popular recently has brought a new wave of stylish Moroccan imports, but there are also plenty of beautiful and inexpensive pierced tin lanterns, sets of tea glasses, textiles, and rugs on offer through homestyle stores and mail-order catalogs.

Exuberant palette

Travel guides for the area and books on Moorish architecture and interiors show this to be a rich mixture of sophisticated building and decoration enhanced by an exuberant ethnic palette.

PROJECT
A painted arch bedhead

COLOR
PALETTE

1

2

YOU WILL NEED:

Deep-blue chalky
finish paint

Pink paint

Deep terra cotta paint

2 x 4in/100mm
squares of thick foam

Star pattern template

Craft knife

Spraymount

Brown wrapping
paper for the
arch template

Scissors

Chalk

Large brush to
apply main color

Small paint brush
for edges

Turn your bedroom into a scene from *A Thousand and One Nights* by painting the walls a warm pink stone color and painting a typically Moorish arch at the bedhead in deep ultramarine blue with a stamped tile surround. Enhance the casbah atmosphere with metal lanterns, candles, urns, and striped woven textiles. All the other colors in the room should be rich and warm so that the effect is one of looking up at an inky blue Moroccan night sky. If this effect appeals to you, why not go one step farther and paint a distant sickle moon and stars on the blue arch shape?

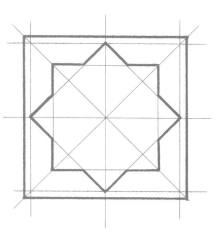

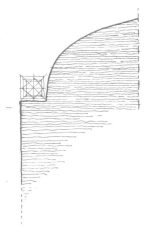

3

COLOR KEY

1 Tangerine

2 Deep ultramarine

3 Palest lemon

TEMPLATE

Draw the star pattern so that it fits neatly into a 4in/100mm square following the method shown in the diagram.

HOW TO DO IT

This arched bedhead does not take long to paint, and the stamped tiles are simple, bold, and effective.

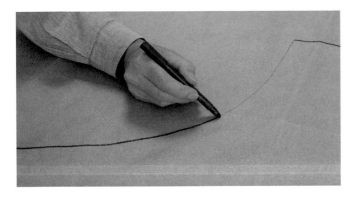

STEP 1 Enlarge and draw one half of the arch pattern onto the brown wrapping paper, either in sections on a photocopier or by squaring up. Cut it out and spray a light coating of Spraymount on one side.

STEP 2 Stick this onto the wall and draw the shape with chalk, then flip the template over and repeat these steps to create a complete arch.

STEP 3 Enlarge the star pattern to 3¼in/80mm wide and stick the pattern onto one of the foam squares. Carefully cut out the shape to the depth of about ⅝in/15mm. Cut outward from the middle every time. Peel off the background to ⅝in/15mm, leaving a star-shaped stamp.

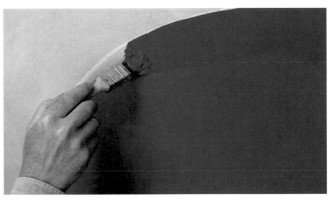

STEP 4 Paint the arch in deep blue, using the small brush for a neat finish around the edges.

STEP 5 Put some of the terra cotta paint onto a plate and coat the square tile stamp. Stamp a tile border around the edge of the arch, leaving the top triangle for now. Leave to dry.

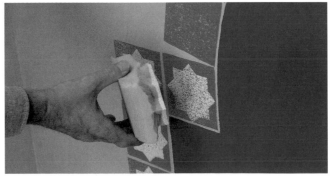

STEP 6 Now coat the star stamp in pink and place one star in every tile shape. Cut a foam stamp in a triangle shape to fill the gap at the top and on each side where the arch meets the straight supporting column. Fill in the gaps with this stamp using the terra cotta color.

India

The subcontinent of India is a huge country of many distinct characters. The Buddhist north is mountainous with a cold climate, and to the west lie the farmlands and deserts of Rajasthan and Gujarat, which border the Arabian Sea. The Hindu south has the hottest climate and the most relaxed lifestyle, and here the economy is based around the traditional creative industries of textile printing and carving. The east has the River Ganges, jungles, mangrove swamps, and Calcutta, the most overpopulated city in India.

There is no such thing as one Indian style, but one thing all the regions have in common is that they mix brilliant colors in ways that break all the Western rules defining "good taste" and color combining! The result is vibrant, energizing, and uniquely Indian. Colors are flung together with great confidence, and their impact is stunning. Different areas of India are famous for their skills in specific crafts such as embroidery, textile printing, pottery, or carpet weaving, but there is no area where most of these traditional skills are not practised anyway.

Brilliant work

It is clear from the dress, homes, and jewelry of the craftspeople who produce these items that they have a genuine love for the patterns, colors, and motifs they reproduce, even though they are poorly paid for the work that they do. Most of the work is produced for the home market. Houses in cities are painted in brilliant colors; temples are adorned with carvings and bronze castings, and each festival generates a hive of industry producing all the necessary deities, offerings, and accessories needed for a proper celebration.

Seeking out the style

Many of the styles we recognize as our own have their origins in India. The paisley shawl, floral chintz, Madras check, Provençal prints, and damask cottons all came from India. Several charities now have Fair Trade arrangements with communities of craftspeople in India who supply goods directly for sale in their downtown shops, so it is really easy to buy genuine handmade accessories, textiles, and ornaments to give a room the right feel.

The sari stores found among the local shops of Asian communities sell lengths of fabric ranging from plain vibrant muslins for everyday wear to the finest exquisitely embroidered cloth for wedding saris. Sari lengths are ideal for draping over curtain poles at windows or as exotic drapes for a four-poster bed.

Most paint companies produce vibrant color ranges. Choose the mainstream flat paints for children's rooms where these brilliant color schemes will always find an appreciative audience; or buy a Mediterranean-style paint that dries to leave an authentic powdery bloom.

PROJECT
Bindi stamps and a border stamp

YOU WILL NEED:

High density foam

Craft knife

Copies of the patterns

Spraymount

Size (special glue)

Small foam roller

Plumb line marked
at 12in/300mm
intervals

2 or more packs of
gold leaf—(the
squares can be cut
in half with scissors
or a craft knife, to
avoid waste)

Very few textiles escape having some extra
form of decoration beyond color dye in
India. It is as if they simply cannot resist
adding another pattern, thread, or ornament.

These little teardrop shapes are inspired by
the decorative marks which Indian women
paint or apply to their foreheads, called *bindi*.

The shape is stamped onto the wall using
a clear glue called gold size, then when it is
almost dry, a sheet of gold leaf is rubbed over
it. The result is a gleaming gold shape. The
pattern for the border is larger and can be
applied either in the same way or with
a bright pink paint color as shown here.

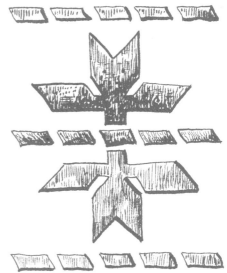

COLOR KEY

1 Deep lavender

2 Lilac

3 Lavender gray

4 Palest lemon

5 Apricot

TEMPLATE
These are the actual size patterns for
the foam stamps and can be traced
from the book. Use thin paper that
will be easily cut through when you
make the stamps.

HOW TO DO IT

Foam stamps can be made from any firm foam, but cutting needs to be done slowly and accurately to get the best effect.

STEP 1 Make copies of the patterns and stick them on the foam. Cut them out carefully, using a craft knife. Practice cutting on an off-cut to judge how much pressure is needed. Cut at an angle so the base of the pattern is wider than the top; this makes the stamp stronger.

STEP 2 Put 1 tablespoon of size on a plate and run the foam roller through it. Coat the *bindi* and stamp it onto the wall at 25in/600mm intervals using the plumb line as a guide. Stamp the next row, starting 12in/300mm from the ceiling to make a half-drop pattern.

STEP 3 Take a sheet of gold leaf with its backing sheet and rub it gently onto the stamped size. The leaf will cling to the size, but easily brush away from the surrounding wall. Don't worry if the motifs are not sharp-edged—this is typical of the hand-blocked style.

STEP 4 Apply size to the border stamp and repeat the pattern along the deep violet band. Complete the whole length of the wall, then apply the sheets of gold leaf. Brush away the excess, then burnish the gold with a soft cloth.

African

The African continent is one of many contrasts, divided in half at the equator by a band of heavy forests. To the north is the massive Sahara desert with the huge countries of Egypt and Sudan. Egypt is one of the great ancient civilizations, whose past is well documented compared to the other African civilizations. In contrast, there are still tribes who lead a Stone Age existence as hunter-gatherers deep in the equatorial forests, or as nomadic huntsmen in the southern deserts.

East Africa borders the Indian Ocean and the Red Sea, and trade with India and the Arab countries over the centuries has made north east Africa more Arab in style than African. There are white domed buildings, minarets, date palms, and bustling markets. Southern Africa has the grasslands, lakes, mountains, and semi-deserts, also wildlife, and people traditionally lived off the land as herdsmen and farmers. Much of Africa's rich heritage of art, crafts, and architecture was undermined by colonization, and only recently has a pride in true African style re-emerged.

Updated traditions

The textiles of West Africa are amazingly varied. Traditional fabric patterns were tie-dyed or patterned using the mud-resist technique, and colored with indigo or other organic plant dyes. Modern dyes are used now, with mixtures of old and new designs. Some of the most interesting feature objects such as bicycles or clocks as design motifs set within traditional border patterns. Utility objects such as baskets, rugs, or pottery remain unchanged. Authentic African goods including textiles and household goods have

been added to beadwork, trinkets, and wood carvings for the export market. The abstract patterns and simple shapes fit in well with contemporary interiors.

African color

The southern African color palette comes from the earth. Red ocher, yellow, burnt orange, and black dominate, with any other available color used to riotous effect. In some places telephone wires are split open and the multicolor wires used to weave baskets; in others tin cans are recycled to make storage trunks, lamps, and toys.

Creating an authentic African-style room should not be difficult or expensive. The look is simple and relies on a few well-chosen objects, shapes, and colors. The walls are roughly textured and painted in bands of color, dark at the bottom and light above. Patterns are loosely geometric and rhythmic. There are specialty stores that deal in African furniture and crafts; baskets, masks, woven wall hangings, and soapstone carvings can be found in some stores and it is also worth exploring flea markets and junk shops for stools, tables, or curios.

PROJECT

African walls

YOU WILL NEED:

Earthy orange, golden yellow, mud brown and warm terra cotta paints in sample size for stencilling

Mat black latex paint (small can)

Short-pile roller

Broad paint brush

1¼in/40mm paint brush

Long rule and spirit level

Pencil

Stencil card

Spraymount

Craft knife

Short, fat stencil brush

The walls in African homes have undulating surfaces that are pitted and rough in places and shiny smooth in others. Smooth walls may need roughing up a bit to achieve the African look. There are several ways to do this. The least expensive is to apply a skim coat of plaster with a wooden trowel, but this is something of a specialized job. A thin, uneven coat of filler can be applied, with a plastering trowel or a large brush, having mixed it 50:50 into white latex paint; or special effect paint, applied with a short-pile roller and given random criss-cross strokes with a decorating brush.

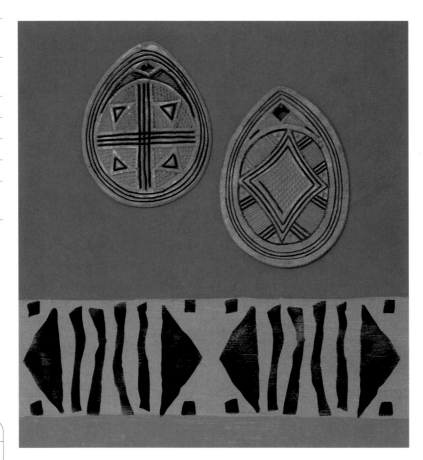

COLOR KEY

1 Earthy orange

2 Golden yellow

3 Mud brown

4 Warm terra cotta

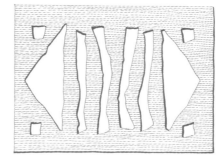

TEMPLATE
This stencil imitates stick printed patterns, so keep the lines irregular when you cut it out.

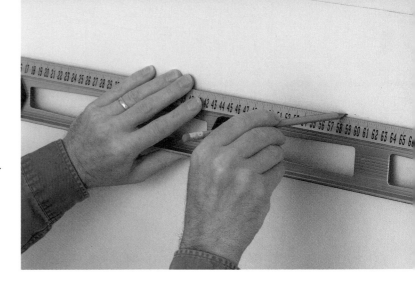

HOW TO DO IT

Stenciling is easy and effective so long as you use Spraymount to hold the stencil in place and remember to use only the smallest amount of paint on your brush.

STEP 1 Measure and mark the wall at 30in/750mm and 3ft/1m height at 3ft/1m intervals around the walls and draw guidelines for the three bands.

STEP 2 Paint the top and bottom parts of the wall first and leave to dry.

STEP 3 Paint the dividing band with your chosen latex paint. Paint the lines freehand using the narrower brush along the edges and filling in with the broader brush.

STEP 4 Cut out the stencil pattern and apply a small amount of Spraymount to the back of it.

STEP 5 Stencil the pattern in the center band in your chosen color.

Miami pastel brights

Miami Beach at the tip of Florida has a style all of its own. The resort was built between the 1920s and 1940s in the Art Deco style, which was popular in New York and Chicago, but in Miami they gave the look a unique twist by choosing a very different range of colors for their buildings. In Miami the buildings were painted with bright tropical pinks, sunny yellows, purples, blues, and greens. The colors were not primaries but bright pastel ice cream colors, perfect for a vacation town.

The buildings echoed the shape of streamlined ocean liners, with the main body of the building painted white and color used to highlight the horizontal banding. For a while Miami was the most glamorous vacation destination, but it fell on hard times in the late 1950s. In the 1980s a massive renovation plan was set in motion, and now Miami outshines its former glory. The buildings are freshly painted and are a little brighter, with less white and more entire buildings painted bright colors; the chrome is polished and neon signs light up the night. The interiors are decorated in a similar style, using colors to stress the geometric devices in the design such as columns, stepped parapets, and windows with narrow horizontal glazing bars. Also synonymous with Miami are palm trees, tropical flowers, nautical themes, flamingos, and unrestrained elegance.

Art Deco Miami-style

Miami is now one of the world's top vacation resorts, and its stylish hotels and boulevards are favorite locations for movies and fashion photography. Creating your own piece of South Beach (SoBe) should not be too hard because a distinctive color scheme will do most of the work for you. Look out for one or two genuine Art Deco pieces of furniture, either from specialized dealers or flea markets.

Miami used Art Deco shapes but applied its own color scheme—you can do the same with bright pastel upholstery. If you have no luck finding original furniture, buy a plain sofa with a streamlined shape and dress it up with contrasting cushions piped in Miami colors.

A touch of fun

Neon lighting is very much a part of the Miami look, and a pair of colored neon tubes would add an authentic glow at night. These can be bought as colored sheaths to fit over standard tubes. Chrome wall or table lights will also fit in well, and there are plenty of good reproduction Art Deco lights around.

Miami has a fun side, and if this appeals to you, then a fake flamingo or two and a few stylized sunset pictures are a must! In Miami, the sun shines all year and most residents are on permanent vacation. Adopt this style at home so that, even if work occupies the day, every evening will feel like a vacation.

PROJECT
Miami deco walls

YOU WILL NEED:

Background color
(choose one of
the three below)
to apply to all wall
surfaces first

Pink, yellow, and
sea green paint

Pencil

Long rule

Spirit level

Plumb line

Paintbrush

Roller and tray

Small foam roller
and tray

Painter's
masking tape

The geometric and streamlined shapes associated with Art Deco can be used mural-style, drawn onto a wall and painted using the Miami palette of tropical bright pastels. The most important lines to emphasize are the horizontals, which should wrap around the room in smooth streamlined stripes. Vertical columns topped off with stepped parapets can be painted around doorways or windows.

Miami is very style-conscious but fun is also high on the agenda, so use the basic shapes and colors but feel free to interpret the style in your own way.

COLOR KEY
1 Lemon curd
2 Deep rose
3 Aqua blue

HOW TO DO IT

Wrapping your walls with these bands of Miami color will liven up any room. It's fun, but don't rush it as the paint needs to be dry before you apply the tape.

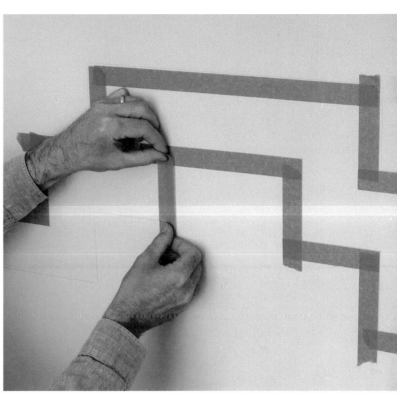

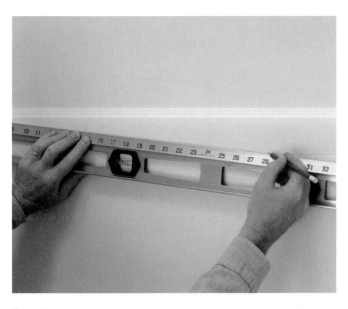

STEP 1 Draw the streamlining stripes by measuring up from the floor, and marking, then drawing pencil lines. Check them with the spirit level.

STEP 2 Run painter's tape around the outside edge of the lines.

STEP 3 Paint the bands of color inside the painter's tape.

STEP 4 Leave until almost dry, then peel off the tape.

Industrial modern

The industrial look is one that was born out of necessity, when young people in big cities like New York, Paris, and London went looking for places to live and found themselves priced out of the market. The empty properties that attracted their attention were dockland warehouses and abandoned factories whose business had long since closed down or moved out of town to escape the traffic-clogged streets. The buildings presented an opportunity for a whole new way of living, and loft style was born.

One of the most essential aspects of industrial modern style is to retain as much of the fabric of the original building and any specialized associated material as possible. A large winch with an iron hook, for instance, would be seen as sculptural and retained, as would a metal staircase, steel shutters, or a ventilation shaft. The idea is to keep the best of the building's original character, but also to make it work as a comfortable home.

Fabulous fittings

Once the factory and warehouse spaces had been colonized, the next step was to make use of factory fittings, office furniture, and items of industrial scale that could be converted for use in the home. Galvanized iron shelving, movable storage units on hefty rubber casters and cafeteria tables were put to immediate use, and aluminum waste bins, metal filing cabinets, catering ovens, and sets of lockers began appearing on the pages of magazines. Floors were covered with aluminum sheeting or painted with industrial paints; brickwork was exposed, and scaffolding poles were used to create mezzanine sleeping decks in the middle of vast open spaces.

Lofts and warehouses have now moved up to the top end of the market – but the industrial modern style is here to stay. Aluminum flooring, stainless steel units, and catering ovens are readily available. There are aluminum and steel acrylic paints that will make any surface look like cool metal, and a range of textured wall covering that looks just like factory flooring. Metal storeroom-type shelving, track lighting, and bare concrete used for seating, tables, shelving supports, and planters are all a part of this pared-down style.

"Islands of comfort" are another vital ingredient—cool hard surfaces look fabulous, but everyone needs to curl up and feel warm and comfortable as well. These comfort zones are furnished with generous leather sofas, soft mohair or lamb's-wool throws, deep pile rugs, and low coffee tables. Even in a vast space, clever lighting can create a sense of intimacy if kept low and concentrated by using floor and table lamps to cast warm pools of light. Use the same basic concepts to create an industrial modern style in any room—keep the style utilitarian and the space cool, open, and uncluttered, but be sure to include soft areas for comfort and indulgence.

PROJECT
Breeze-block shelving

YOU WILL NEED:

6 cinderblocks

2 x 14in x 6ft x
¼in/350mm x 2m
x 20mm planks

Primer

Mat black paint

Paint brush

Concrete cinderblocks have replaced bricks as the basic construction material in many new houses these days. They are regular-sized, strong, and inexpensive, but they don't make beautiful looking walls, so bricks are still used as a facing material. The rough gray texture of the blocks takes on a more sculptural quality when taken out of context and used indoors as shelf supports.

The planks used here are painted black wood but other materials would also look good. Glass, steel mesh, or galvanized zinc are all very much a part of the industrial modern style.

COLOR KEY

1 Mushroom brown

2 Mid-gray

3 Palest lemon

4 Pale mushroom

HOW TO DO IT

The sculptural style of this shelving unit relies on the positioning of the cinderblocks. Use a set square to align each one at the correct angle.

STEP 1 Apply a coat of primer to the shelving planks. Leave to dry, then apply two coats of black paint.

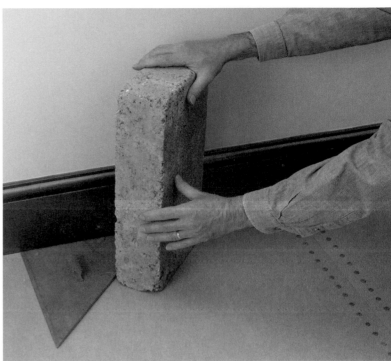

STEP 2 Space two base cinderblocks to stand 2¼in/60mm from the wall, 20in/500mm apart, angled at 45° to the wall. Stand the first shelf on top with 10in/250mm overlap at each end.

STEP 3 Place two more blocks on the shelf above the lower ones, this time angled at 90°, the narrow side facing forward.

STEP 4 Stand the second shelf on top, again with 10in/250mm overlap at each end, and position the final two blocks angled at 45°. Put the third shelf on top. Note: this shelving unit should only be used in rooms with solid floors and where it is unlikely to be knocked.

Urban minimalist

COLOR
PALETTE

The key elements for this look are open space, good color, and only a few well-designed pieces of furniture. Floors are left bare with either painted or waxed floorboards. Ornaments are out—instead, choose really stylish utility objects which are sculptural in their own right. We all need radiators, but the urban minimalist goes for fabulous columns, swirls, or ladder-style "rads." Everything makes a style statement, and for this look you really do have to maintain a disciplined attitude to tidiness, because clutter is definitely out.

The furniture can be from any period so long as it is in good condition and has a design pedigree—some of the most contemporary looking chairs and loungers were actually designed in the 1920s by the famous community of designers at the Bauhaus in Germany. Chairs from any of the key decades in the last century can be reupholstered in plain contemporary colors to flatter their shape. Brand new technology sits comfortably alongside retro pieces, so long as the good design ethos remains paramount.

Urban color

Light interiors are always enhanced when a good proportion of white is used, as it reflects and doubles the room's natural light. Leave windows bare when possible and paint window frames and surrounds white. If the windows are small, then create the impression of bigger windows by painting a broad white border beyond the frames and below the sill down to floor level, which will create the impression of full length windows. Folding wooden shutters look wonderful, but if they are likely to blow the budget, choose plain white shades instead.

The urban minimalist look consists of just a few equally important elements, and color is one of them. Consider the room's function and any existing color that appears in furnishings, paintings, or accessories when choosing a wall color.

Adding accents

A meditative lavender or pale powder blue creates a relaxing atmosphere in a living room, and pale mushroom brown looks good with white and deeper browns, especially if bright colors such as spring green or red are used for upholstery. Just one or two permanent colors are needed, and others can be added as color accents with cushions, vases, or flower arrangements.

Fresh flowers are very much a part of the urban minimalist look, and a whole new style of floristry has emerged to complement it. Single variety arrangements or indoor plants are favored, such as vibrantly red or orange dahlias in tall glass tubes; rows of pink orchids growing in moss-covered containers; zinc tubs planted with white marguerites, or a huge earthenware pot filled with tall wild grasses.

PROJECT
Making a bolster cushion

YOU WILL NEED:

A bolster cushion pad

Rough silk fabric in a bold color—enough to wrap around the body of the bolster plus two circles for the ends. Cut them to allow for a ⅝in/15mm seam

Matching thread

Piping cord (cut a strip of fabric and fold it over the cord, then stitch close to the cord using the zipper foot, and clip along the seam allowance so the cord bends easily into a curve)

A zipper to fit length

Scissors

Pins

Sewing machine

A bright silk bolster cushion on a sofa or chair can be used to add an accent of color to the room. Bolsters are long, firm tubular cushions whose shape and proportions suit the minimalist look. They were a popular feature of the design-conscious Regency and Biedermeier styles in the 19th century, and Le Corbusier's famous leather and chrome lounger has a bolster neckrest, which certainly confers it with top design credentials.

The secret of success is to take the sewing slowly so that you keep turning the fabric in a smooth curve.

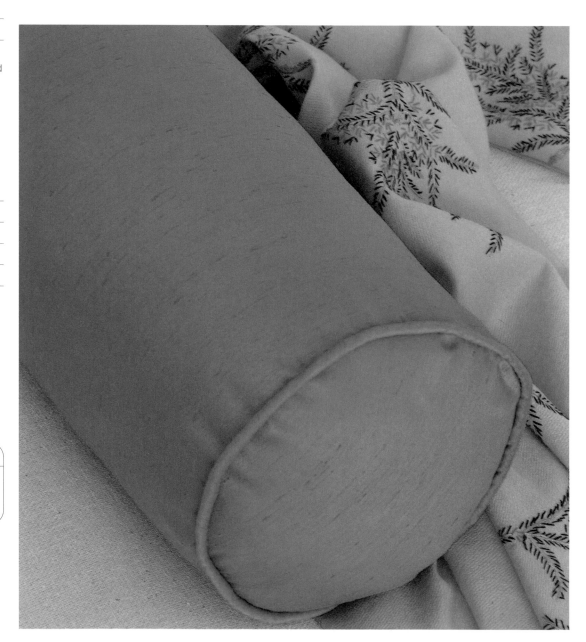

COLOR KEY

1 Soft emerald

2 Fawn

3 Deep golden yellow

HOW TO DO IT

Fit a zipper foot to the sewing machine so that you can stitch up close to the piping and the zipper.

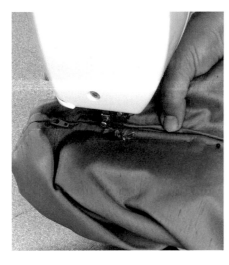

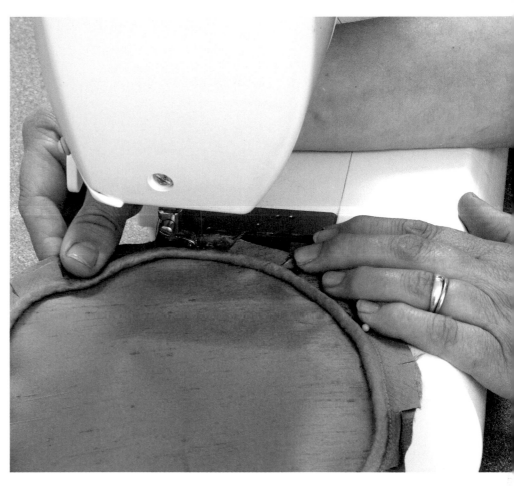

STEP 1 Turn over a small hem and stitch the zipper into the seam of the main body fabric. Undo the zipper so you can work on the cover.

STEP 2 Sew the piping onto the round ends before you stitch them to the main body.

STEP 3 Snip out ³⁄₈in/10mm notches every 1¼in/30mm around the end pieces. Pin the ends in place and stitch them using the zipper foot to get close up to the piping cord.

STEP 4 Press the seams lightly and turn the right side out. Fit the cushion pad inside and close the zipper.

Index

A

accents 90
additive color 12
African style 78–81
aluminum 28, 86
ambient lighting 20
anaglypta 28
appliqué drapes 7, 64–5
arches 70, 72–3
Art Deco 15, 82, 84–5

B

bamboo 26, 29
bathrooms 32
Bauhaus 90
bedheads 72–3
bedrooms 14, 32, 52, 60, 72–3
beige 13, 36
bindi stamps 7, 76–7
black 10, 13, 36, 42, 78
blinds 32, 36, 48–51, 90
blue 6, 10, 13–15, 18–19
    design 23
    highlights 58, 66, 70
    style 90
    textures 36
bolster cushions 52, 92–3
border stamps 76–7
breeze-block shelving 88–9
brown 17, 19, 36, 58, 90

C

carpets 16, 24
casbah style 70–3
ceilings 18–19, 22, 25, 36, 58
chair rails 18, 23, 28
chemicals 24
children 14, 20, 22, 62, 74
chrome 29, 32, 36, 82, 92
clashes 12
clutter 32, 40, 86, 90
co-ordination 16, 49, 53
cold colors 13
color wheel 10–11
complementary colors 12
concealed lights 20
concrete 28, 88–9
contrast 13, 23, 32, 34, 50, 68

cork 29
cotton 17, 58, 74
crafts 74, 78
cream 13, 17, 23, 36, 58
Cubism 15
curtains 7, 32
    highlights 48–52, 58, 62, 64–5, 74
    textures 38–9
cushions 25, 36, 49, 52–3
    highlights 58, 60, 70
    style 90, 92–3

D

3-D effects 40–3
dark colors 13, 18
design principles 8–25
designers 15, 16, 47
dimmer switches 20
discords 12
dragging 30
drapes 36, 38–9, 48, 50–1, 74
drop-shadows 19, 40

E

effects 6, 30–1, 40–3, 80
emulsion 17, 29, 74, 80
English Country style 7, 58–61

F

fabrics 16, 22, 24
    highlights 48–51, 53, 58, 60, 74, 78
    textures 26, 32, 38–9
factories 86
Fair Trade 74
fashion 15–16, 51, 52
favorites 8, 15
felt 7, 28, 64–5
felt appliqué curtains 7, 64–5
fittings 86
floors 22–3, 25, 32, 36, 54–5, 70
flowers 36, 47, 62, 82, 90
focus 46–7
four-poster beds 32, 74
front doors 14
furniture 16, 29, 32, 36
    highlights 49, 58, 60, 66, 78, 82
    style 86, 90

G

geometric patterns 23, 29, 34, 70, 78, 82
glass 17, 21, 88, 90
gloss 17, 22, 34, 58
gray 12–13, 32, 36, 42
green 6, 10, 13–14, 17, 19
    highlights 58, 70
    style 90
    textures 36

H

hallways 14, 22, 28, 66
harmonies 13, 50
high ceilings 18
highlights 7, 44, 46–55
historical styles 22, 56
hot colors 13
hue 13

I

illusion 6, 19, 22, 40, 62
Indian style 7, 74–7
industrial modern style 28, 86–9
intensity 13

K

kitchens 14, 62, 66

L

lamps 18, 20, 25
    highlights 52, 60, 66, 78
    style 86
Le Corbusier 92
leather 17, 29, 36, 70, 86, 92
light colors 18, 21
lighting 18, 20–1, 25, 36
    highlights 58, 82
    style 86
linen 17, 26, 29, 36
living rooms 40, 42
loft style 86
long rooms 19
low ceilings 18, 58

M

magazines 15, 22, 46, 86
matting 17, 36
mat 17, 22, 32, 34

Miami style 82–5
minimalist style 90–3
mirrors 58, 60
modern style 29, 86–9
moldings 19, 28, 40
Moorish style 7, 70–3
Morocco 70, 72
mud-resist technique 78
muslin 36, 48, 52, 60, 74

N
narrow rooms 19
neon lights 36, 82
nets 48, 52
neutrals 13, 23
    design 25
    textures 36–9, 44, 51, 53
Newton, Isaac 10
night clubs 20

O
offices 86
open-plan style 19
orange 6, 10, 13–14, 23, 78

P
paint 13, 16, 23, 30–1, 36, 46
painted floors 54–5
painted wall finish 68–9
painted-arch bedhead 72–3
paneling 32, 42–3, 58
pastels 13, 15, 82, 84
pattern 16, 18, 22–3, 25
    highlights 50, 53, 58, 62, 64, 70, 78
    textures 28, 30, 36
period styles 22
personal taste 8, 14–15
perspective 40
picture rails 28, 58
pictures 25, 46, 82
pigment 13, 15, 66
pipework 19
planning 8, 22–3
plants 36, 46, 47, 66
plaster 19, 26
    highlights 58, 66, 80
    textures 28, 40
plumb lines 34, 35, 43

primary colors 6, 10, 13, 42, 68
proportion 18, 36, 41, 50, 58, 90

R
raffia 26
red 6, 10, 13, 17, 19
    highlights 58, 78
    style 90
reeds 29
regional styles 22
remnants 53
Roman blinds 50–1
Romany style 7, 62–5
rose-stenciled wall 60–1
rugs 23, 25, 32, 36
    highlights 46–7, 52, 58, 66, 70, 78
    style 86

S
sample pots 24
sash windows 23
satinwood paint 23
saturation 13, 44
sculpture 46–7, 86, 88–9
secondary colors 6, 10
selection factors 22
semigloss paint 23
shades 13, 32–5
sheepskin 17, 32
shelving 25, 86, 88–9
shutters 32, 66, 86
simplicity 41
sisal matting 17
skirting boards 23, 28
soft furnishings 25, 36, 52–3
specialist ranges 24, 54, 78, 82
spectrum 10, 13
sponging 30–1
spotlights 20, 47
stained floorboards 23
stairways 22, 28
stamps 7, 76–7
stenciling 19, 30–1
    highlights 46, 58, 60–1, 81
    textures 34–5
styles 7, 86–93
surface color 13
swatch boards 24–5

T
templates 34, 38, 40, 60, 64, 72, 76, 80
terminology 12–13
terra cotta 17, 66, 70
tertiary colors 10
texture 6, 16–17, 22, 25
    effects 26, 28–9, 32, 34, 36
    highlights 68
    style 86, 88
throws 36, 52, 86
tiles 32, 66, 70, 72–3
tricks 18, 20
trompe l'oeil 40
Tuscan style 7, 66–9

U
uplighters 18, 20
urban minimalist style 90–3

V
vases 25, 47, 60, 90
violet 6, 10, 13
visualization 14, 46

W
wallpaper 22, 23, 24, 26, 29, 61
walls 19, 22, 25
    highlights 46, 50, 58, 60–1, 66, 68–70, 80–1, 84–5
    textures 32, 35–6, 40, 42–3
white 10, 13, 18, 21
    highlights 58, 70
    light 12, 13
    style 90
    textures 32–6
window treatments 48–51
windows 21, 23, 32, 38–9
    highlights 58, 62, 66
wood 17, 29, 32
woodgraining 30
woodwork 22, 25, 32, 36
work areas 20, 28

Y
yellow 6, 10, 13–14, 21, 23
    highlights 66, 78
    textures 36

Acknowledgments

The publishers would like to thank the following for use of copyright material:

Laura Ashley Limited: pp. 28, 45, 49(t), 50, 51(b), 52, 53(b), 53(br).

Elizabeth Whiting Associates: 3, 6, 7, 9, 13, 15(m), 15(tr), 18, 19, 20(t), 20(b), 21(t), 21(b), 22, 25, 29(t), 29(b), 48, 49(b), 51(t).

b = bottom, br = bottom right, m = middle, tr = top right, t = top.